The Partisan's Coat

A Historical Novel by
Yehiel Grenimann

Mazo Publishers

The Partisan's Coat

ISBN: 978-1-956381-50-4

Contact the Author:
www.farawayfromwhere.com
Email: thepartisancoat@gmail.com

Published by:
Mazo Publishers
www.mazopublishers.com
Email: info@mazopublishers.com

Cover artwork by:
Nehama Grenimann Bauch
www.illuminatedfragments.com
Email: nammyg@gmail.com

■■■

This is a work of fiction. Some of the characters and incidents are based on real people and events, but the names have been changed. There is no claim to historical accuracy in the details.

The poem by Avrom Sutzkever on page 3 is reproduced by permission of the translator. (Translated from the Yiddish by Richard J. Fein), from *"The Full Pomegranate"*, Poems of Avrom Sutzkever, p. 154 (2019, State University of New York).

Who will last, what will last? A wind will last.
The blind will die, their blindness last.
The ocean's raveled foam will last.
A cloud snagged by a tree will last.

Who will last, what will last? A syllable will last,
As creation seeds again and lasts.
For its own sake, a fiddle rose will last.
Seven blades of grass that know the rose will last.

Longer than all the northern stars will last,
The star that falls in a tear will last.
In the jug, a drop of wine will last.
Who will last, what will last? God will last.

Isn't that enough for you?

Avrom Sutzkever

CONTENTS

ACKNOWLEDGMENTS

My thanks go, first of all, to Debbie, my beloved wife and companion of more than forty years, whose love nurtures me and whose passion for life, learning and literature (and skill as an editor!) are a constant source of inspiration. Some of the important plot ideas and subtle aspects of the characterizations were hers, crystallized in discussion with her about the book.

I also wish to thank my four children, Nehama, Neriya, Benny, and David, for their support and encouragement, and the whole family for their love and patience through the process. A special thank you to my talented daughter Nehama for the cover art and design. My brothers, Sam and Jack Green, are always there supporting me in spirit when I sit down to write, as are the memory, inspiration and heroic lives of my parents, Boris and Chana Green, of blessed memory.

I am grateful to my childhood friends Avi Cytrynowksi and Zev Wagen, who are intimately acquainted with the experiences that served as an initial source of my creativity. Each read the manuscript, gave important insights and were supportive of the writing process. Avi also contributed some invaluable editing of the text.

My cherished Jerusalem friends Mordechai Goldberg, Elliot (Yisrael) Cohen and Margalit Jakob-Frutkoff each read the manuscript at different stages and encouraged me to persevere and complete it. I thank Gary Ginsberg, David and Bev Young, Haim Watzman and Sara Avitzour for their supportive friendship and shared concerns and for accompanying me on parts of the journey into writing a second novel. We share the commitments to religious and humanist values with which my main character, Joe, struggles throughout the narrative, as well as our complex relationships with the miraculous but crazy country we live in.

I must also mention my wonderful Yiddish class at the local Talpiot community centre in Jerusalem, led by Eudice

Winer Harris. It was a source of enrichment, friendship, and aesthetic pleasure, and it helped reconnect me to my roots in the destroyed world of Yanosh, Eva, Rivka and Bora, and to my Yiddish-speaking childhood. Many of the participants grew up, like me, in the homes of Holocaust survivors. In a sense, Joe's story is also theirs.

This book is dedicated to

Suzanne Bino (née Green/Grenimann) of blessed memory,
only daughter of my father's only surviving brother, Fima

John Adler of blessed memory, my wife's cousin

Daniel Avitzour of blessed memory, my dear friend

all of whom loved life, art, music, and literature.

Each in their own way inspired me and enriched me on my personal journey. I cherish their memories and remain grateful for having known them.

Prologue
FULFILLING THE PROMISE

Yanosh and Eva Kaminski were survivors of the horrific war that upended Jewish life, the likes of which the world never knew. Fortunately, they had some non-Jewish friends who had hidden them outside of the Warsaw Ghetto.

After World War II ended, they were relocated to a displaced persons camp in Germany.

In one of the first signs of the rebirth of Jewish tradition, Yanosh and Eva celebrated their marriage, under a chuppah. It had been thirteen long years since they spoke of marriage in Pilsudski Square, Warsaw, under the old oak tree.

They could not stay in Europe any longer, certainly not in Germany. Many of their friends went to Palestine, others to America. This was the question they faced and had to decide together: Where would their new home be?

After sorting out all their concerns and considerations, they chose Australia. It was very far away from Europe, and as unwanted Jews, they were lucky to get a visa to anywhere at all.

In 1946, with passage booked, they boarded a ship – destination Fremantle, Western Australia. The ship journey was long and difficult, particularly for Eva, who was pregnant. While strolling on deck amongst the many passengers, they were surprised to run into a man they knew. It was Bora – an ex-partisan with a hazy past who had gotten them out of trouble after the war.

Not long after this encounter with the only person they knew on the ship, they heard that someone had been murdered. They were shocked to find out that the victim was Bora – they watched in disbelief as the ship's captain buried Bora's body at sea.

■■■

Soon after their arrival in Australia, Eva gave birth to a daughter, whom they named Lily, after Eva's mother, who was murdered in Treblinka. Their son Joseph (Joey) was born in Melbourne three years later, not long after they arrived there from Adelaide. They shortened their family name to Kamens and did their best to adjust to their new country.

■■■

Ten years later...

Yanosh and Eva have established themselves in a quiet suburb of Melbourne. As they try to forget their traumatic past, their second child Joey (later Joe) sets out on a journey of his own...

Part 1
MELBOURNE, AUSTRALIA

Chapter 1

THE COAT

Joe Kamens stared into the glass case. The thick fur collar, the tan colour, the length, the deep pockets, the buttons… it was the same coat!

Here in the partisan warfare section of the military museum in Minsk – a memento of the Soviet struggle against the Fascist invaders.

He remembered how, as a boy of ten, he first found the coat in Melbourne, in the winter of 1959.

■■■

Joey liked to hang out in the backyard, in the windowless little family shed. No one could see him when he was inside. It was quiet there, and safe. He didn't mind the musty smell.

He would go to escape his parents' arguments when they were home, and to keep away from Lily, his irritating older sister, when he was left alone with her. He'd heard them argue about the clutter in the shed, his mother yelling at his father to "throw away some of that junk", but he was glad he hadn't. Joey loved to imagine stories about the old things he'd find.

Apart from the old clothes, he played with the tool kit, wore his daddy's big rubber boots, created shadow puppets on the shed wall waving his hands in front of his electric torch. Joey made himself a cubby hole with some wooden boxes. He left crumbs of bread to attract company and observed the creatures crawling around in the shadows – beetles, snails, spiders. He loved watching them to discover their hidden world. Once he saw a mouse scamper across the floor, its long tail slithering under the door as it escaped. He'd been told to stay away from "that dirty shed" but he kept going back. It was his special place.

One late afternoon, poking around the shed, the glint of a metal handle caught Joey's eye. The handle peeked out from under old blankets. Joe yanked out a brown suitcase, and it fell to the floor, raising a cloud of dust that made him sneeze.

The locked lid of the suitcase didn't respond to his efforts to pry it open. He went over to his father's out-of-bounds tool kit, took out a screwdriver, and stuck it in the lock. A few jiggles later he heard a click. He opened it! He returned the screwdriver, glancing outside to check that no one was nearby. Leaving the door ajar, he went back to check his find.

The open suitcase revealed more old clothes: a big old coat, a pair of pants, some shirts. Joey emptied the contents onto the ground. A small black notebook fell onto the pile. He picked it up. Something fluttered out and fell back to the ground – a yellowed newspaper clipping.

Joey picked up the paper. He saw the familiar name Hitler above a photo of marching soldiers, and a map of Europe with arrows marked across it. Unable to understand the words, he folded it, slid it back into the notebook and flipped through the pages. There were more newspaper clippings with photos and writing in a foreign language. He thought it might be Polish.

He found a pair of worn black shoes, with a cloth bag in one of them. It jingled. A treasure!

Joey poured out the contents of the bag.

Disappointment.

Only old medals, in a foreign language, not money!

The letters were strange. He saw the Communist symbol, the red Soviet star, recognized it from the magazine his father sometimes read. The one his mummy didn't like.

A date was inscribed on one of the medals – 1945. The year the war ended! There was a swastika in one of the photographs, on the ground under a soldier's boot.

His imagination lit up.

Communists, Nazis, the war... his parents' stories.

Joey turned back to the coat and looked at it. It had a fur collar. He shook off some dust and tried it on. It was big – way too big – and warm, and it had deep pockets. He put the bag in one of them and looked more closely at the suitcase. On the inside of the lid there was writing.

He wiped away the dust. His nose was itchy again, hit by a musty smell, but he stopped the sneeze coming. He didn't want to get caught in the shed.

He read:

Janusz Kaminski – Ul. Nisca 10, Warszawa

Daddy's name, he said to himself, *before he changed the family name to Kamens. Must be his address. It's from Warsaw. That's where he's from.*

Joey heard footsteps. He was scared. He was supposed to be practicing violin. He didn't want to be yelled at or punished. He'd already put the screwdriver back.

He stuffed the clothes, except the coat, back inside the suitcase, closed it and shoved it under a pile of blankets on the lowest shelf. Just in time.

The door creaked and opened. His mother's slender silhouette in the doorway. A hand clicked the switch on. A light bulb hanging from the ceiling shone a circle of pink illumination on her normally stern, thin face. Eva was wearing her red shawl. Joey could see the light's reflection in her glasses, the glint of her Star of David pendant as it moved in and out of the light with her breathing. He couldn't see her eyes, couldn't tell if she was angry.

"Joey, what are you doing in here?"

"Just playing." He straightened in front of the suitcase to conceal it.

"What are you wearing?"

"A coat I found. It's warm and has great pockets!"

"Let me look at it."

Joey handed it to his mother. She ran her hands over the fur, putting her hands in the pockets. Joey watched worried, wondering what was coming.

She laughed, waved a lock of hair out of her eyes. "You want to wear this dirty old thing? It needs to be cleaned... It's much too big for you."

Joey made a face but knew things weren't so bad after all.

"Oh, all right, I guess you can keep it, but I will clean it for you." She was smiling. Then she gave it back. "You can keep it if you want."

He smiled too, hugging the rolled up coat like a big teddy bear. Eva turned off the light as they left the shed.

"Bring the coat inside with you. Put it in the laundry. And then come to the kitchen, Joey. It's time for tea."

Joey emerged to see the last glimmers of sunset. It was cold. He went into the house clutching his new coat, noticing the hands on the kitchen clock as he came in. It was almost six o'clock.

The next morning before school, before his parents woke up, Joey crept into the kitchen. The red clock on the wall showed ten to seven as he passed under it into the pantry. He took the electric torch from the cupboard as quietly as he could. He went out into the backyard and opened the shed door. Flicking on the torch, he saw its light reflected from the metal handle that was sticking out from a pile of things. He pulled down the suitcase and opened it, this time without any problem. Inside, under the clothes, was the notebook.

Joey took out the notebook and turned the pages. It felt dry and fragile. He saw a picture of a uniformed man standing on a stage surrounded by flags, talking to a crowd.

He read "29 Maj, 1939". He could work out that date, but he didn't understand the other Polish words.

That's the month of May in Polish, and the year is when the war started. It's May 1959 now, so this is just twenty years old... ten years older than I am.

■■■

Sunday morning, a week later...

It was a cold day, wind whistling through the electric poles and rain hitting the front windows of their weatherboard home. Joey felt bad that he hadn't told his mum about the things he'd found. He decided to ask his mother about the suitcase and its contents, his curiosity overcoming his fear.

Eva was sitting in the kitchen, drinking tea and reading the Yiddish newspaper. Joey waited for her to look at him, but she didn't. He gathered courage to speak:

"Mummy. Mummy…"

She looked up at him.

"What is it?"

"I want to ask you something."

"Go ahead."

"Remember when I was playing out in the shed last week..."

"Uh ha... You looked silly in that old coat... much too big for you."

Eva had gone back to reading her newspaper.

"Mummy, listen!"

Eva looked up again, looking at Joey through her thick glasses, her big green eyes peering at him as if he were in an aquarium. He didn't like that look. Something was wrong. After a long silence she responded:

"I'm listening, Joey."

He wasn't sure he still wanted to ask her, maybe he could back out of this conversation now, but no, he couldn't stop talking. He felt like a fish about to be caught in a net.

"I found a suitcase in the shed... The fur coat was in there..."

Eva stared hard at him, folded her newspaper, and put it down.

"And an old newspaper clipping. It had a date on it, May 1939... and... and some old medals, one from 1945. It's stuff from... from... the time of the war, isn't it?"

"A suitcase? Was it brown with a metal handle?"

Joey nodded, hoping this was not going to mean punishment.

"I've told you not to rummage around in the shed, haven't I? There are dangerous things in there, your father's tools. Daddy would be furious if he heard that you'd touched them. You haven't, have you?"

He shook his head vigorously, knowing that if he told the truth he would be in bad trouble with his dad. Silence again. Joey waited, but wanted to run away. She was thinking about what to tell him, he could see that in her eyes.

"Yes. It's from the time of the war. Daddy wouldn't let me throw that old suitcase away... It's been sitting in the shed for years. That coat... the stuff in the suitcase... was Bora's."

"Who was Bora?"

"You don't remember? We've talked about him, haven't we?"

"No."

There was a strange look in his mother's eyes, as if she were faraway, not there opposite him, then she said: "It's a long story, Joey. I'll tell you about it all some other time; I need some peace and quiet now."

"So, it's OK for me to look through that stuff?"

Joey heard parakeets chattering in the white eucalyptus outside the kitchen window, waiting for his mother to answer.

"I suppose it's all right, but..."

"What's the matter?"

"Nothing, darling, it's all right."

But Joey had again noticed that look in her eyes. He decided to leave her alone.

"Thanks, Mummy!"

Joey tried to sound cheerful. He left the kitchen to go watch television in the living room. He was happy Lily wasn't home so he could now watch his favourite show. He was watching Jet Jackson when his mum marched into the room:

"Turn that thing off! You are supposed to practice violin now!"

Joey knew he was already in trouble because he was caught in the shed. He didn't want her to take away his precious fur coat or find out about his other new-found treasures. He pulled out his music sheets and the violin his daddy had brought home weeks before. He started playing his scales.

Eva left the room, smiling to herself.

After that, Joey began to play with the medals he'd stored in his room, imagining he was a freedom fighter resisting the Germans. He'd wear one each time as part of his game. They were inscribed in letters he couldn't read, but he knew they were from wartime Europe. His make-believe became more real. Lily wouldn't play with him. She wasn't interested in what he was doing.

Joey loved wearing the coat, carrying books, pencils and notebooks in those wonderful pockets.

One morning he discovered a hole in one side of the coat; his searching finger went right through the thick fur lining to the rough exterior.

"This is a bullet hole!" he said to himself, wondering if Bora was wounded in the leg?

■■■

A week later, one evening he heard his mother talking in the kitchen with her best friend, Mrs. Ruben, the lady with the double chin.

Joey didn't like Mrs. Ruben much. He hated how she would pinch his cheeks and comment: "Your Joey should've been a girl vit dos rosy cheeks und curly hair!"

She smelled of garlic. Uggh. And he saw that her husband Yoseleh had blue numbers tattooed on his arm. His mother warned him not to ask about the numbers or stare at them. That only made him stare more, ignoring his mother's disapproving look.

Joey heard Bora's name; he came over to the kitchen door and listened. They were talking in Yiddish.

"I'm telling you, Betty, Yanosh first met Bora, the famous partisan fighter, right after the war. By that time, he was a smuggler who helped Jewish refugees like us cross borders." The clock above the kitchen door was ticking loudly. Joey moved closer to the door to hear better.

"...to get out of Poland?"

Tick tock, tick tock...

"Yes."

Tick tock, tick tock...

"It was terribly cold that year."

Tick tock...

"Yanosh showed me a coat Bora had given him, a fur coat he'd worn during the war. It was so cold that year. Yanosh was grateful..."

The clock was annoying. It was hard to hear them.

Tick tock, tick tock! Tick tock!

"A partisan coat from the war?"

Joey almost cried out when he heard that. *Wow, it's a real partisan coat!*

"Yes. It is... We were fleeing Poland from the Communists.

Bora helped us escape; they intended to kill Yanosh."

"*People wanted to kill Daddy?*"

Tick tock, tick tock!

"Why?" Mrs Ruben asked.

Joey wanted to smash the clock to stop its relentless ticking noise. He thought he heard sobs, he wasn't sure. Eva's voice sounded strange as she answered:

"The Communists were taking control of Poland, they started assassinating activists. My husband was on their list."

"Really? Yanosh? But he doesn't seem the type."

"Maybe not now, but Yanosh was active in the nationalist underground and Bora…"

Joey couldn't hear the end of his mother's sentence!

"Really? You owed your lives to this man Bora. Did you stay in contact after that?"

"Listen Betty. It's a long story. I've got to prepare dinner before Yanosh gets home. He has a temper, you know."

Joey remembered how his father once smashed dishes, his mother crying, he and Lily scared huddling in the next room waiting for their fight to end.

He heard them getting up, the clinking of things being placed on a tray. He moved away from the door. Just in time. His head was buzzing with all this weird information about Bora, Polish undergrounds, Bora the partisan smuggler.

"I've got to go, but I'd like to hear more about Bora."

"Next time. Please, Betty, keep what I told you to yourself. Yanosh shouldn't know we talked about it."

"You're right… Don't worry, Eva, you can trust me."

They walked past Joey to the front door. Mrs. Ruben gave him a pat on the head as she passed. He cringed at her touch. He was sure they didn't know he'd been listening to them. They kissed and parted.

As he walked down the corridor to his room, he heard Lily listening to music in her room. It was the song "Catch a Falling Star." She was always listening to dumb stuff like that.

Joey didn't understand everything he'd overheard his mum saying about the past, but he wanted to know more. He'd started reading about the war in Europe.

One day, Yanosh came home with a surprise gift for the family, an encyclopedia that he'd bought on installments. It was a set of big red books that Joey enjoyed leafing through, looking for pictures of exotic fish and brightly coloured birds. Now it was going to help him understand about the war too! He kept asking his parents lots of questions, but they didn't tell him much and got annoyed at him. Reading books about the war in the school library helped. The librarian commented to Yanosh and Eva on the change in his reading habits. He'd mostly read books about animals and nature until then. His teachers told him they were impressed with his growing knowledge of European geography and recent history. Until then, he had been the best in his class when it came to knowing about sea life and unusual birds and animals, now he was becoming a history expert too. Lily, and other kids at school, teased him for being a "know-it-all", but he didn't care. He liked to know things, as much as he could.

Joey began to put together a picture of that mysterious war for himself. He had trouble understanding some things, but he did now know more about the battles, and that the Nazis had done some very bad things, especially to Jews. Six million was an enormous number. He hated being told "you will understand when you are older". He wanted to know now.

The day after overhearing his mother's conversation with Mrs. Ruben he asked his sister, Lily, if she knew about Bora. Lily wasn't always nice to him, but she knew things he didn't know. Maybe she knew more about Bora.

She was sitting in her room curled into the corner of her bed under her Elvis poster, reading. He barged in on her, and she asked, annoyed:

"What do you want, Joey? Ya' oughta knock, you brat!"

"Sorry, I wanted to talk about something. It's important..."

Joey fidgeted, dancing on one foot, then the other, waiting for her to look at him.

"Lily, please..."

Lily studied him over her thick-rimmed glasses. Her green eyes looked bigger when she wore them, but looked small now. She put down her book and smiled before speaking.

"OK, shoot. What's your excitement about this time? Why don't you sit down? Here," she said, pointing to her bed.

She sounded almost nice for a change. Joey sat down on her bouncy bed.

"I heard Mummy talking with Mrs. Ruben. Yesterday. They were talking about this guy Bora."

"Bora? Yes. Why?"

"Mummy told Mrs. Ruben that they owed their lives to this man Bora."

"Yeah, I've heard of him. He was a friend of Dad's after the war. Something like that. Anyway, why are you asking me? And stop jumping around like that, you'll break the bed in a minute!"

"Because of the coat I found in the shed. Mummy told me it was Bora's. He was a partisan, you know, and that coat is a real partisan coat!"

Lily banged the bedside table hard.

"Joey, don't be silly. I've seen you wearing that great big fur coat. You look ridiculous in it! And stop being a nuisance!"

She glared at him.

"But it's great to play with. The coat even has a real bullet hole in it!"

"You're being stupid, Joey! Now leave me alone."

Joey was sorry he'd asked her. She was no help at all. He hated his stupid older sister and her dumb friends! He slammed the door behind him.

■■■

A week later he overheard his mum talking to Mrs. Ruben. They were talking in the living room while he was next door in the kitchen. He heard his mother's raspy voice:

"Bora... Nazis... ship to Australia... the Aurora... Bora... shots... dead... buried at sea..."

Joey came closer to the door to hear better. He could smell

the cigarettes; the smoke came up at him from under the door.

"He was murdered on the ship."

"What?"

"Yes. The murderer was never caught."

Joey couldn't hear everything they said this time. He was too scared to listen by the door any longer. He might sneeze from the smoke, so he moved away.

This sounded like exciting stuff. Wow. Bora was part of a murder mystery. But it's a taboo subject... and he wanted to know more, but how could he? No one told him anything! They all had secrets.

He knew he couldn't ask his father. He never had time to talk to him, always busy.

He started wearing the coat to school on chilly days, his books in the pockets. Yanosh and Eva were concerned about their ten-year-old's obsession with the history of the war years. His classroom teacher, Charlotte, called to ask about the old coat he was wearing to school, told his parents that he had been acting strangely lately, asking a lot of questions about the Second World War. Joey was annoyed that she'd called. None of her business.

A few days later, Joey came into the kitchen holding an old photo.

"What do you have there, Joey? "

"Is this him? Is this Bora?"

His mother looked at the photograph. It was a face framed by a half-circle of dark curls, a large bald pate, bicycle-spoke wrinkles around small penetrating eyes; the man had a slight smile and was wearing a coat with a fur collar. Joey studied her eyes in anticipation.

"Yes, that's him." She did not look pleased.

"And there's the coat!" he said, triumphantly.

"Yes, that's the coat."

Yanosh was often cloistered after work in his study, writing. Eva would complain to him that he didn't spend time with Joey. One evening after dinner, Joey asked his mother to have his hair cut short "like the other boys in school." He was surprised when

Yanosh looked at him from over his Polish newspaper, smiling, the sides of his moustache arching up as he spoke:

"I'll take him. Needed. Agreed. He looks like an unshorn sheep."

Eva and Lily laughed.

"Baaa," Joey joked.

"I'll take him to the Carlisle Street barbershop tomorrow after work, all right?"

"Thanks, Daddy!"

Yanosh took him to the barber the next day as he'd promised. Joey saw his school friend Adam leaving when they came into the steamy shop. They waved. He climbed up onto the chair, had a cloth tucked around his neck. It prickled. He smelled eucalyptus oil as the barber started cutting. He watched in the mirror as the man cut his curls and they fell to the floor.

Now I'll look like a regular Aussie schoolboy.

Joey noticed a tattooed blue number on the inside of the man's muscular, hairy arm. He couldn't stop staring as it went back and forth across his vision.

He'd caught glimpses of numbers on the arms of his parents' friends before, knew they had been in a camp ("dos laager", they called it) but he'd never seen the numbers so close. He shuddered, imagining what the man must have been through in the war.

"Joey, you shouldn't stare at the barber's number like that," his father told him outside the shop, "or at our friends' either. It's rude."

"It's from the Germans, isn't it? He was in a concentration camp."

"Yes. He was in Auschwitz. He cut off hair there." Joey looked up at his father's stern face. "People who were in those places don't want to be reminded. You've got to be sensitive to that."

"I won't do it again."

That Saturday after his haircut, Yanosh took Joey down to the beach.

Joey loved going to St. Kilda beach. They hopped on a tram near the intersection of Carlisle Street and Hotham Road. It rattled down to Luna Park, just past Ackland Street. They got off and walked past the Palais Theatre, Joey struggling to keep up with his fast-walking dad. Joey rolled down the grassy slope that led down to the sandy shore of St. Kilda beach. His dad laughed watching him. Joey wasn't used to his dad cheerful like this, but it didn't last. Soon they were walking along the sand in silence, his father looking into the distance as he often did.

Joe could see around the bay. The city and its towers were on the right, looking out to sea, the expanse of suburbs along the coast on his left. He could spot boats out on the water: yachts, speedboats, fishing boats, even diminutive rowboats bobbing up and down on the gentle waves. Further out, he could see an ocean liner or a big cargo ship. Port Phillip was a protected body of water.

They strolled along a long wooden wharf. The kiosk was open. His dad bought him an ice cream, bought himself a beer. Men stood along the pier, fishing. He could smell their sweat, beer and cigarettes. They were silent, but occasionally Joey heard someone let out a sigh or a sharp curse. Joe could hear the recurring sound of waves underneath, hitting the wooden supports of the peer or lapping the shore.

"You want to know more about the war, Joey, huh?" Yanosh asked his son, relighting his pipe.

Joey nodded, but wasn't sure he wanted to hear what his father was going to say.

"I think you're not old enough to understand, son. It was a terrible time. We were lucky to survive it all. You should appreciate what you have, growing up here in a free country."

Joey didn't know whether to ask about Bora and the coat. His father's tone didn't invite more questions, so he didn't ask.

"Do you understand what I'm telling you, Joey?"

"Yes, Daddy," he muttered and took another lick of his ice cream before it melted.

"OK. Let's head home."

Chapter 2
DROR, THE JEWISH YOUTH CLUB

On Sunday mornings Joey liked to sleep in. He tried to ignore his dad's weekly invitation to join him outside working in the garden. He hated it when his dad woke him early on days when there was no school. He curled up under the blankets and went back to sleep. Yanosh's heavy silence while working unnerved him. After a family lunch, his dad would cloister himself with his books through the afternoon. His mum and Lily usually visited with friends. Joey watched sports on TV.

One day in June his mum took him aside. She told him that this Sunday he'd come with her to somewhere special. He didn't like the sound of that.

"Where do you want to take me, Mummy? I'm happy at home on the weekend."

"But Joey, you spend too much time alone at home. You ought to go out and meet other children. You don't play with your sister, and you've only one friend at school. You'll see. You will like it."

They boarded a bus to Glenhuntly Road, got off at the corner of Hotham Street and waited for a tram. Joey looked around. He saw a mezuzah on several doors. He smelled a bakery, then saw the familiar sign of Asher's kosher bakery across the road. He'd enjoyed eating bagels there one late Sunday morning with his mum and Lily. He'd have been happy to go there again, but they didn't cross the road.

"Isn't this the way to the Goldsteins?"

"I'm taking you to a Jewish club called Dror, near there. I'll be visiting them while you're with the other kids. That name, Dror, is a Hebrew word and means Liberty in English. It is part of the Zionist youth movement."

"A Jewish club? Zionist youth movement? Do I have to go? Why don't you make Lily go?"

"Lily has her own friends already."

"I've got a friend too! You know… Adam. I could go to his place instead."

"Joey, you agreed. I'm sure you'll have a good time." She sounded annoyed.

Eva took his hand and, pulling him along behind her, began to walk up the hill. She led him past a kosher restaurant, a tailor's shop, and a small Indian restaurant. When they reached Gordon Street, she turned left, Joey followed. They walked past the Esquire Theatre and continued until they reached the police station next to the wooden railway bridge. They crossed the road, went through a rusty green gate and entered a large yard, framed by a row of bushes.

Joey felt dust in his nostrils, then sneezed. He heard shouting, screaming, laughter of children.

"Gimme that ball!"

"It's my turn!"

"Not fair!"

Kids were running everywhere. Big ones and small, boys and girls, some were kicking a football, others skipping rope, a few were meandering around without any clear direction. Joey saw groups of three and four, pairs, and lone individuals, and a big group of boys arguing by what looked like a football goal. It was dusty and noisy.

A redheaded older boy with freckles was yelling at a group of younger kids, trying to herd them towards a building. A bell began clanging loudly. Joey saw a big girl in a bright red dress standing on a veranda energetically ringing the bell with both hands. Kids began running inside. The yard was transformed within minutes. Mayhem dissolved; an orphaned cloud of dust remained in the yard.

Joey saw a red-roofed wood building with a door and window shutters painted green. The paint was peeling in places. A wide veranda skirted the entrance where the girl in the red dress had rung her bell. In the far corner of this veranda, he saw older children sitting in a circle. Some were fidgeting, others talking while waiting there. An empty chair beside a small blackboard in the centre of the circle was his clue that they awaited their leader.

Sunlight began to fade. Sunset brought with it a reddish-orange tinge to the sky above the building. Lights began to twinkle on inside.

The redhead greeted them, ushering them in. The guy's broad smile emphasized the freckles around his warm brown eyes.

"Shalom! My name is David. Welcome to Dror headquarters!" he said.

They followed him into the building.

"This is Joey. He's ten years old, in fifth grade at school," his mother said.

"That's a good age to start at Dror. Welcome, Joey. We'd love to have you join us here on Sundays."

"How long until I have to come back to pick him up?" Eva asked.

"Be back just before six."

"Bye, Joey. Enjoy yourself! I loved my youth movement in Warsaw when I was a girl."

Joe felt his mum's sadness when she said Warsaw.

"Was Bora in a youth movement like you?"

"That's a strange question Joey. No, I don't think so but... I've got to go. Have fun here. Bye!"

His mother bent over to give him a quick kiss on the forehead. She let go of his hand and stepped away. Joey watched as she left, could hear her footsteps on the wooden veranda. He wished his mummy would stay longer but she walked away fast. He saw her through the window growing smaller as she strode away without looking back. On his own now.

"Com'on, Joey," David said, "I'll take you to Evelyn's group. You'll like her. She's a great madricha! It's Hebrew. It means group leader."

Joey was puzzled for a moment.

"Ah... I remember now... mummy told me about a madrich she had in Warsaw... his name was Mordechai Antilewich."

"Anilewicz." David corrected him, "Yes, I've heard of him, of course."

David took his hand and led him along a narrow corridor. Joey could hear children singing in a strange language. Some of the doors were open. He peeked in as they walked past. Each had an older youth in the front surrounded by younger children.

Joey saw a group dancing in a circle to accordion music.

At the end of the corridor, they walked through a little white room, full of shelves and cardboard containers bulging with drawing materials, paper, glue. They passed a cluttered notice board and continued down a couple of steps into a wide rectangular-shaped back room.

The walls, painted yellow and blue, were adorned with nature pictures, slogans, children's drawings. Paper mâchés hung, some swinging, from one side of the slanting ceiling. The entire back wall facing him was a sliding glass door. He could see through it out into a backyard where children were playing cricket by a fig tree.

David let go of his hand, and smiling, introduced him to a young woman with glasses perched halfway down a pointy nose.

"Joey, this is Evelyn."

"Hello Joey!"

"A new boy for our group!" she announced, loudly. "Welcome to Amelim, Elsternwick, Joey."

Joey squirmed, wished he could hide but managed to smile back at her.

"You can sit down over there next to Zev," she whispered to him, patting him on the shoulder.

Joey sat down on a cushion on the floor next to a plump, bespectacled boy. He began hugging himself as he looked about him at the other kids. Zev gave him a friendly nod, one of the girls looked his way and smiled briefly, but the rest, having stopped staring at him, now ignored him.

He felt very alone.

The day's sun was waning, but the soft light, still coming in through the picture window, danced on the faces around him.

The children looked happy, except Zev, who despite his first friendly smile, looked sad.

Evelyn picked up a book, sat down, and started reading to the group. She had a soft, melodic voice.

"In Degania, south of the Sea of Galilee where the Jordan river flows, the halutzim, that's Hebrew for pioneers, would gather after a long day's work in the fields."

Evelyn turned the book around to show them a photo of a lake, then a photo of people in shorts, wearing floppy hats, and dancing in a circle.

"They're dancing the hora," she explained.

Joey was bored by this. He wasn't the only one. A couple of kids were dozing. Zev pinched the girl sitting on the other side of him. She didn't cry out, just poked him back, hard. He stopped pinching her. Evelyn didn't notice, continued reading:

"Degania was a kibbutz," she explained, straightening her glasses.

Joey knew that word from his parents.

"My mum has friends on a kibbutz!" he called out, the other kids staring at him as he said his first words there.

"That's very nice, Joey, or should we call you Yossi. Maybe you can tell us more about that sometime, but not now." The other kids laughed, except Zev, who gave him a sympathetic glance.

"The word kibbutz is Hebrew for a collective settlement or commune," she explained. "It was the first one. Here, we're like a kibbutz," she went on, "and I hope one day you'll be one of the halutzim, like them."

Joey had stopped listening. He wasn't happy to have been silenced just when he'd found the courage to say something in front of the group. He didn't like being laughed at either.

Evelyn gave out a sheet with Hebrew words on it. She taught them the song:

"Hine Ma Tov Umah Naim Shevet Achim Gam Yachad."

She translated: "How good and pleasant it is for brothers and sisters to sit together."

He liked the singing, saw that the kids were enjoying it too.

It was better than listening to that boring book she'd read to them before.

They went outside to play a game. They pretended to be members of that first kibbutz. They dug holes, planted saplings and watered them in the yard to "reclaim the Land". They played other fun games until dark.

On the way home, he told his mother about the afternoon spent in that back sunroom, and in the yard by the fig tree.

"It was fun," he told her. "A girl called Judy won the game we played. She was the last one left in the square. She moved so fast no one could hit her with the ball."

"I played that same game in Hashomer Hatzair in Warsaw. It was called Machanayim."

She squeezed his hand as they walked on, but she was no longer smiling. Her eyes were moist and red.

"What's the matter, mummy?"

"It's nothing, Joey. I'm just remembering some of my childhood friends."

"Mummy?"

"They're all dead... the children I played with... gone... killed by the Germans... in the war."

"I know about that. The Germans killed a lot of Jews, mummy, I know."

"They were bad... evil... so were many of the Polish people. They killed Jews who escaped the Germans or turned them in to be killed."

"But you told me you were hidden by Poles; they protected you from the Germans, didn't they?"

"Yes. They did, but they were protecting us from the other Poles too."

His mother's face was pale, her eyes remote. Joey tried to hug her, but she pushed him away.

"Mummy, mummy?"

"I can't, Joey. Not now."

Joey stopped asking questions. He saw he was making his mother unhappy. His enthusiasm was gone. He was now feeling sad, and very alone. He knew he shouldn't ask again.

Later in the evening, sitting in the living room with his dad deep in his Polish newspaper, his mum, knitting, and his sister Lily, looking at pictures in a glossy magazine, he told everyone the story of Kibbutz Degania and the pioneers. His father put down his newspaper to listen to him. Yanosh's pipe was emitting smoke at an angle from the side of his mouth, giving their living room a pleasant scent of oranges and spice. Eva continued knitting, but listened too. Lily ignored them.

"We know people who live on a kibbutz," Yanosh told him, but he already knew that. The next thing his dad told him he'd never heard before:

"It's called Lochamei HaGetaot, which means the Ghetto Fighters' kibbutz. They went there after the war to join friends who had been in the same Zionist youth movement."

"So why didn't you go too? Why did you come to Australia instead?"

"We wanted to be free, to start a new life without wars and we didn't think immigrating to a country where another people didn't want to be overrun by Jews was a good idea. It was obvious to me there was going to be a war there."

"Which people, Daddy?"

"The Arabs. They were the majority in the country."

"I'd like to go live there, to help the Jewish halutzim build our country!" he said, looking up at his father. Yanosh had a strange smile on his lips.

"You see what you've done, Eva! We have a ten-year-old Zionist in the house now!"

Eva and Lily laughed.

Joey didn't understand what was funny, felt hurt by the conversation, got up to go to his room.

"When you're older, Joey, maybe we'll go visit together. Some day. I have some old friends there I'd like to see again," Eva said wistfully.

"Did Bora live on that kibbutz?" Joey asked.

Yanosh looked over at him, drumming his fingers on the table...

"Bora!? No. We told you. Bora is... dead. Stop asking about him. We're sick of hearing his name from you all the time!" Yanosh said.

"Oh. All right. Sorry."

"And why are you still wearing that old coat all the time?" his mother asked. "It's not so cold today."

Joey ran to his room, slamming the door behind him. He stretched out on his bed, trying to muffle his crying.

Chapter 3
Contacts in Israel: Eva and Rivka

The first one to go to Israel from among his family and friends was his mother. Eva had planned the trip for a long time. She had rediscovered her old friend Rivka reading an article about life in Israel in "The Jewish News".

The journalist interviewed members of Kibbutz Lochamei HaGetaot. Eva hadn't known that Rivka was a member. The article reported that Rivka Avrami, originally from Warsaw, had lost her entire family in the Holocaust. She had been in a D.P. camp in Germany, crossed the Alps, and then met her future husband Motti in Italy after the war.

Together, they had challenged the British blockade, coming to Palestine "illegally", before the creation of the State, and had fought in the War of Independence. Motti, badly wounded, had survived the fierce battles but with a disability for the rest of his life. They married and had just one son, but now they had lost that son, Oded, in battle. "Tragedy after tragedy", the journalist commented.

"Rivka! Oy, poor Rivka!" Joey heard his mother exclaim, then start crying. That evening she told Yanosh about it, showing him the newspaper piece.

"It's sad. We were right to immigrate to Australia." Yanosh commented.

Eva nodded in agreement. Joe wasn't so sure.

"You should write to your old friend," Yanosh said.

"I will."

Joey looked at the paper too. He saw a black and white picture of a woman with her family, all smiling next to a tractor decorated for a festival. The caption called it Shavuot, the festival of weeks. The man in the picture only had one arm.

Rivka's only boy, Oded, had been killed in a skirmish with Arab Fedayeen near the border with the Gaza Strip. Eva wrote to the kibbutz central committee to express her condolences. Rivka's reply arrived in the post a few weeks later.

His mother read that letter, repeatedly, tears in her eyes. Rivka wrote that she was happy to hear from Eva after so many years, that she missed her, that her letter was timely. They started corresponding.

Joey saw his mum's eyes light up whenever a letter arrived from Israel. Eva started sending parcels to her kibbutz friend. He would come with her to the post office when she sent them. She filled the parcels with his and his sister's old clothes, but also added a new item of clothing each time. He would watch as she removed labels, rumpled up a shirt or pants, then added them to the parcel of old clothes.

One of Rivka's letters brought a surprise.

"Bora is alive!"

Joe overheard them talking excitedly. Their voices were raised. He heard his dad say that the funeral at sea had been a trick, that "the body" thrown into the ocean had not been a corpse at all, that the Zionist underground had paid off the ship's captain. Bora, having carried out his mission in Australia, had returned to Palestine and had participated in the War of Independence there as an officer in the Hagana.

"He always was a clever, tricky bastard," his mother commented.

"Yes, he was. He fooled everyone!" his father said, chuckling.

Joe didn't fully follow what this was all about, but he did understand that this Bora must be a special guy. He decided that day that he must meet him. He would look for him in Israel. He would bring him back his special coat.

That year, Joe and his new friend, Charlie started attending bar mitzvah classes. His best friend, Adam, didn't come. Adam's parents had decided on a perfunctory ceremony at the Reform temple.

Joey's mother supported that and encouraged him, but the bar mitzvah itself never happened. His father opposed the ceremony.

"None of that religious mumbo jumbo for my son!" Yanosh yelled when Eva brought up the subject.

"But, Daddy, all the other boys are having bar mitzvahs this year. Why can't I?"

"Joey, you can have a party if you want, but no need to go to the synagogue. Why should we pay to have you taught by those religious fanatics to recite meaningless words in a language you don't understand, to a Divinity we don't believe in?"

"Yanosh, they are not fanatics. He ought to know something about his tradition," Eva pleaded.

"You read so much, Joey you can add some reading about Jewish history and tradition, no?"

Joe nodded, but was disappointed.

"Anyway Eva, you've already brought him to Dror. He learns things there. We don't need a ritual as well. He meets Jewish kids there, that's plenty."

Eva smiled at hearing that her husband at least accepted Dror.

"I will buy him a book of Jewish history – something balanced and objective – for his birthday. I'm not discussing this anymore!"

Joey started going to the bar mitzvah classes with his mum's help, despite his dad's disapproval.

The story of heroic David the warrior shepherd was his favourite. He loved the illustration of little David with his slingshot in hand, standing over a felled Goliath in the textbook they studied.

He thought of Bora and his heroism when he saw that picture. He'd been told that Bora was a little guy too. When a few years later, in 1967, little Israel beat three Arab armies in a war that lasted only six days, he thought of little David and his slingshot, and he wondered whether Bora had been part of that fighting. He was proud to be a Jew after that war.

One time, as they sat learning the Torah cantillation, Reverend Davies stopped the class to relate to the content of what they were reading. It was Exodus, the story of the slavery in Egypt and the bravery of Shifra and Puah, the two midwives who resisted Pharaoh. These God-fearing women did not carry out Pharaoh's order to kill all the first-born male babies.

Dr. Davies pointed out the ambiguity of the text regarding the midwives' ethnic origins. Were these midwives Hebrews or Egyptians? The medieval commentator, Rashi, said they were Hebrews, but another commentator called Aberbanel said they were Egyptians. He asked them what they thought was the correct interpretation of the verse.

Charlie thought they were Hebrews, emphasizing what he thought was the simple meaning of the words, "Hebrew midwives". Joe thought of them as brave Egyptian women. He was convinced that Pharaoh wouldn't give such an order to Jewish women.

The idea that there were righteous gentiles who stood up to that evil in ancient times and risked their lives to save Jews matched his mother's stories about those Poles who had helped Jews in the war. He was aware that his parents owed their lives to such people.

Most of the kids agreed with Charlie, but Joe stuck to his understanding, stubbornly.

Joe was inspired by this story. He imagined Judy as one of the Egyptian midwives, saving babies and defying Pharaoh would be in character for her. He imagined them wrapping babies in a coat like his partisan coat and smuggling them away, just as Bora had brought Jews from the ghettos to the safety of the forests, and later, smuggled Polish Jews across borders away from the antisemites of Eastern Europe.

Chapter 4
UNITED BOYS' HIGH SCHOOL

Joe enrolled in United High; an exclusive State high school modelled on British grammar schools. His friends Adam and Charlie also went to United.

The school building sat on a hill above the Yarra River, a castle-like structure surrounded by well-watered green playing fields. Once filled with the sounds of the Cockney and Irish English of British immigrant children in class, it now reverberated with a cacophony of voices in immigrant English: Jewish children using Yiddish expressions in their English, but also kids of Greek, East European, Lebanese origin whose English carried those rhythms.

Alexander, from a religious family of Russian origin, wore a black yarmulke when eating his daily kosher lunch. Other kids taunted him, throwing coins at him and chanting:

"Jew! Jew!"

"You Jews love money!"

"Go live in Israel!"

Joe burned with rage and humiliation when he saw what was happening.

What would a partisan like Bora do? Defend Jewish honour, of course! That's what I'll do.

He decided to sit with Alexander and convinced his Dror friends to join him; he told them Jews should stand up for themselves and Adam and Charlie started sitting there too. Joe picked up and threw coins back at the antisemites and he and his friends gave them threatening looks, invited them to a fight after school. No one showed up, and the taunting stopped. Joe learned to admire Alexander's quiet pride through all this, enjoyed talking to him about science. They became friends.

In May 1967, Nasser, the Egyptian ruler threatened Israel with war, demanding the UN withdraw Sinai peace-keeping forces stationed between Israel and Egypt, which they did, and massing tanks and troops near the Israeli border. Israel called up its reserves, waiting for the attack. Joe's parents attended emergency public meetings of the Jewish community and talked about the danger to little Israel surrounded by belligerent Arab States. Joe was surprised to see how much even his father cared about the country. Alexander started reciting Psalms, explaining to Joe that that's what his parents and religious Jews all over the world were then doing in their synagogues. Joe doubted that would help. Everyone was worried.

Joe had been given a transistor radio as a bar mitzvah gift. He dug it out of his desk drawer, started listening to the news, and brought it to school like many of his friends. They'd gather around at lunch time to listen. The non-Jewish boys who had mocked Alex before, returned to make fun of them:

"Don't worry Yids, soon the Arabs will finish off the Jews!" Joe heard one of them yell one day, while the others laughed.

"They'll build gas chambers for you all, like the Germans did!" another kid shouted.

Joe was furious, but remained silent. Charlie lunged into the crowd of jeering, chanting taunters, throwing punches in every direction. Adam and Joe pulled him out, bleeding.

The bullying boys suddenly dispersed. A teacher appeared.

"What's going on here?" he asked, staring at Charlie's bleeding nose.

They were silent.

"You. Go to the nurse, and then report to me outside the principal's office. The rest of you come with me now!"

As no one was willing to tell him what had happened, he placed all the Jewish boys, including Charlie, in detention for the week. Nothing happened to the bullies. Joe and his friends were outraged at the injustice.

Joe heard rumours about a fist fight in the staff room. One of the science teachers, a sarcastic guy whom they were all scared of, had said something antisemitic, and Shlomi Meyerson, the only Jewish teacher in the school, had punched him so hard that he'd broken his nose. Shlomi became an overnight hero in the eyes of the Jewish boys. He'd defended their honour.

During the first week of June, in a pre-emptive strike, Israel defeated the Arabs in just six days. The taunting stopped, Alexander started wearing his yarmulke all the time, the numbers at Dror meetings increased and, during the cold winter days that year, Joe started wearing his partisan coat again.

He became a madrich in Dror, instructing the younger kids about the ideals of the kibbutzim, and singing the latest Israeli songs. He imagined himself a soldier.

Shlomi, their new-found hero, left for Israel. He'd been the only Jewish teacher at the school. Now he was gone; he'd skipped the country because he was wanted for police investigation for assault. He never came back to Melbourne.

Chapter 5

1970: First Visit to Israel

Joe aced his matriculation exams. He topped the school in biology and was awarded a prize. Yanosh and Eva came to the Caulfield town hall graduation, glowing with pride. Lily couldn't come because she had a university exam the next morning, but she baked him a cake to honour his achievement.

Ugh. Typical Lily.

When he returned to his seat, his prize book in hand, his mother greeted him with a kiss, then his smiling father turned to him and asked:

"So now, Joey, you can apply to medical school, can't you? I think, with your marks, you won't have any trouble being accepted. You've done so well!"

"Umm, yeah, Daddy, you're right. I probably would be accepted to medicine if I wanted to. I've thought about that a lot. I'm not sure yet what I want to do, but... but... I was thinking of going to Israel for a year in the Dror program, to spend time on a kibbutz. That would give me time to think."

Yanosh's smile had disappeared as Joe spoke.

"What! No, you can't do that, Joe! Listen to me. A year in Israel would be a big mistake."

"But Dad..."

"Don't interrupt me! You should get on with your studies, advance while you still can. You have opportunities we never had... No, I won't agree to a postponement for a whole year! You can forget about that right away, Joey!"

"My name is Joe," he mumbled, overwhelmed by his father's anger.

"Your son has chutzpah!" Yanosh said loudly to Eva.

Eva, in a whisper, said, "Lower your voice, Yanosh! You're disturbing people. We can talk about this at home."

Eva was still smiling. Joe and Yanosh were not.

Joe lay in bed angry that night, thinking.

Dad is being horrible. He won't listen to me. I'm not going to do what he wants. It's my life!

He heard his parents arguing about him in their bedroom. Couldn't sleep.

He didn't join Judy, Charlie and Adam for the year in Israel. They wrote to him about their kibbutz, about trips all over the country, filled him in with their group gossip. He burned with resentment at his father, was jealous of his friends, but heeded his mother's advice and kept it to himself, but he didn't go to medical school.

He applied for natural sciences with a major in biology, was accepted at Monash University and started studying there. Monash was known for its radical activism, but he focused on his science in the new lecture halls and well-equipped labs of an institution that reminded him more of a modern factory than a school.

Joe overheard them arguing about him again.

They never argue about Lily. Why doesn't Dad get off my back!

He heard his mother say: "Let him be. He can always switch to medical studies later if he changes his mind."

"He's stubborn..."

"Like you, Yanosh..."

"I don't think he'll ever study medicine..."

"We'll see about that!"

Joe plugged his ears with earphones to listen to Bob Dylan's song, *It Ain't Me Babe*, and continued swotting for his biochemistry exam.

His midterm exam results, casually left on the dining room table, delighted his parents, but they also revived his father's nagging about medical school.

"Joey, brilliant results! Now you can go study medicine!"

Not that again.

"Would you consider doing that, Joey?"

"OK... OK... I'll apply if you'll finance a trip to Israel this summer as you promised. And stop calling me Joey!"

Yanosh and Eva were surprised, brought out a bottle of vodka in celebration.

Joe had no intention of studying medicine, but if a promise would get him a trip to Israel, he'd make it. He wanted to see the country for himself, wondered if he could trace Bora. He'd bring the coat with him. Maybe the coat would help him find Bora.

The year ended. Joe applied and was accepted to Medicine at Monash University. He set out for Israel in a student program called "Israel Academy", financed by his father.

In that year, 1970, he first met Steve, a young Canadian student. They met in the shuk in Jerusalem's old city. They drank strong coffee together in a small Arab coffee shop that Steve knew. Joe visited him in the student dorms. Joe first smoked marijuana in Steve's room. They talked about their Jewish identity, about religion and God, about the Vietnam war, about girls. Joe told his friend that he was considering coming back to live in Israel. They agreed that before Joe's return to Melbourne they'd go down to Eilat together to go diving there.

That visit to Eilat created a strong bond between them that continued in regular correspondence after Joe's return to Australia. They hung out with two blond Swedish girls they'd seen sunburning red on the sand, their bikini tops beside them. They splashed them with cold water to gawk at their bouncing boobs when they jumped up. The angry girls quickly clad and left, leaving the two horny guys disappointed. They bumped into them again the next morning. They all laughed about the day before, the girls accepted their invitation to have a beer together after a swim and they spent a couple of happy days together. Joe was no longer a virgin.

The diving was a wonderful experience. Steve rented gear. They swam around the coral reef observing multi-coloured, luminous fish, and other strange sea creatures. Joe later decided to specialize in Marine Biology, inspired by that experience. He was fascinated by what he had seen: the starfish, an octopus, the dolphins. Joe imagined spending time up in the Great Barrier Reef when he got home.

Joe had fun that summer and saw a side of Israel he'd never been told about.

He visited Rivka on her kibbutz up north. The tall, sad lady was gracious, as was her war invalid husband, Motti.

Their kibbutz apartment was cosy, the walls lined with books and artwork which reminded him of home. She brought out lemonade and a chocolate cake which was delicious.

"You can feel at home here, Joey. Your mother and I are good friends," Rivka said, her husband nodding.

"I know," but Joe felt foreign and was very aware of the gap between them.

They're Israelis, I'm Australian. They've suffered wars, I haven't and... the elephant in the room – I know they've lost a son.

His Hebrew was poor, but their English was excellent. Language was not a problem, but conversation was difficult. It faltered on small talk until he gathered the courage to ask:

"I want to contact a man who helped my parents after the war."

"A man? Who? What man?" Motti asked.

"Joseph Borowski. My parents told me you know him. I heard he's still alive here in Israel. I'd like to meet him."

"Ah, Bora. Yes, we know him, Yossi, but he comes and goes, like the desert wind." Rivka said.

"But you wrote to my parents that you met him, didn't you?"

"Yes, I did, but that was five years ago. He isn't in the country now. Away on a mission."

Joe was disappointed, wondering what this meant. What kind of mission? Mysterious.

He felt awkward being hugged and kissed by these foreigners and was happy when he could leave to get back to his group after his short visit with them.

Motti left the room, Joe was sitting alone with Rivka. He'd tried not to stare at the black-framed picture of their dead son, but Rivka noticed.

"That's my late son, Oded. You remind me of him, Yossi."

"I do?"

"Yes. His eyes were dark, dreamy brown like yours."

Joe didn't know what to say, or how to say it.

"I'm sorry."

She accompanied him back to the group's tour bus.

"If I hear something more about Bora I will contact your group leader," she promised. "And send my love to your mother please, Joey!"

Rivka accompanied him back to the Holocaust Museum entrance where he rejoined his friends. He reluctantly entered the museum. He had skipped the tour of the kibbutz to visit Rivka, having arranged to meet the group here.

Although he already knew a lot about the Holocaust, nothing could have prepared him for what happened next. As he was exiting the exhibition, he heard screaming. It was a woman's voice. When the rest of the group emerged, he learned what had happened.

One of the group, Ilana, had screamed inside the section about the Auschwitz extermination camp. She explained in tears that she'd seen a familiar face inside – in the picture of Jews being herded into the gas chamber. It was her grandmother, whom she recognized from her mother's picture of her in their living room in Melbourne.

One of the faces I just saw in there might have been of one of my grandparents. I'll never know, I've never seen photos of them. At least Ilana knows what her grandmother looked like.

A bitter blessing.

His tour group also went to Yad Vashem. Hidden away in a forest on the edge of Jerusalem, the museum was on a hill with beautiful views of the city. The contrast between this view and the scenes inside the museum was shocking. In the auditorium they watched a French film called "Night and Fog". He closed his eyes to some of the images on the screen.

He tried to find out more about Bora. He filled in a query form there at the research centre, having talked to the lady at the information desk about partisans. He asked her and their guide about a partisan officer called Joseph Borowski, but neither knew the name nor could they tell him anything. In the section on partisan warfare, he studied the faces, but none looked like the photo of Bora he'd found as a kid.

The trip was intense. He came home confused about Israel. He realized that it was important for Jews to have a country of their own after the Holocaust, that there was a strong religious connection to the Land of Israel, but nowhere had he really felt at home there. It was so strange and foreign, nothing like his comfortable home in Caulfield. He wasn't sure he could live in Israel, but he wanted to try. His Eilat experience left him with a taste for more.

Israel isn't only about the Holocaust and Zionism. Real people live real lives here.

Chapter 6

THE YOM KIPPUR WAR

A war started in the Middle East that October. Charlie immediately got up and left to volunteer in Israel. Joe considered doing so but decided to finish his studies first. Larry, always so critical of Israel, surprised him in his support for the country under attack. His anxiety about the situation after the Arabs' surprise attack on Yom Kippur, and his sudden attendance at Jewish rallies in support of Israel were touching. When Larry climbed up to the podium of the student forum and spoke in front of a crowded public meeting about Israel's right to defend itself, Joe found it moving.

He's right, Israel needs our support but it's not enough to make speeches now. Maybe Charlie did the right thing... but... but... I can't go now... not yet... I want to finish my degree first.

Joe spoke to Larry afterwards.

"Larry, good onya! That was great, took courage but I didn't know you were such an ardent Zionist."

"I'm not, but someone had to stand up and say something after all those antisemitic comments against Israel."

"That Maoist who said someone should drop an Atom bomb on Israel was pretty extreme, but you took him seriously?"

"Yes. I do."

"He's a wacko."

"Hitler was a wacko, and you know what happened, Joe. Jews should never again make the mistake of ignoring crazies like him. And anyway, he wasn't the only one shouting hate slogans about the Zionists and their link to American imperialism, as if Israel hadn't just been attacked."

"But I thought you had the same approach!"

"No, I don't. I think Israel needs all the support it can get today. After the war we can get back to being critical, not now."

"I agree with that. I've... I've decided... I'm going to go there and pitch in. I'm leaving right after my final exams."

"Now it's my turn to be surprised. That's brave, but be

46

careful, Joe."

Joe told his parents about his plan to go to Israel soon and help. Both Eva and Yanosh were opposed, tried to talk some sense into him, but to no avail. Eva was stunned, but Yanosh, speaking for both, Eva nodding in agreement said:

"If you want to drop everything and run to Israel now, you'll get no financial help from me, Joe. You'll have to earn the money yourself and then if you still want to go ahead with your crazy plan, that's your business. But we came here to Australia to get away from wars, and to escape extremist ideologies. They've brought the world so much sorrow and death. You should appreciate what you have here in Australia. It's a good country, and you have a home here far away from all that madness over there."

"But Dad... you've gotta understand... as a Jew my place is over there fighting for Jewish freedom! How can you ignore what's happening in Israel now? Don't you care? After everything you and Mum went through in Poland, how can you not care!"

"Of course, we care, Joe. I'm no Zionist, as you know, but I did donate to the emergency fund for Israel. I hope there'll be a ceasefire soon. Too many people have died. Joe, I don't want to talk about this anymore. You're a good student. Find a job, make some money, and then you can make your own decisions, but don't expect me to pay for this or support you throwing your life away like that."

Yanosh stormed off, mumbling to himself. "Ungrateful kid... Eva... I should have put my foot down sooner about that Dror involvement."

He turned and glared back at Eva as he entered his study.

"Yanosh, stay! Calm down... please."

The study door slammed shut behind him. Eva led Joe into the kitchen and whispered to him:

"Joey, I understand how you feel. I hear your passion but think carefully about it. It's a big step to take. It's dangerous over there. If you really want to go, I'll help you, give you some money and write to my friend Rivka to help you when you're there. Don't tell your father. And don't talk to him about this again. Just decide, and then we'll work it out. But why don't you just wait until this war ends; we can arrange a visit over there together, after you've established yourself here."

"Thanks, Mum, but no, I've got to go. I'll be OK. Don't worry so much. I'm not a baby anymore."

She caressed his head, kissed him, and left the room to placate her angry husband.

Joe sat down at the kitchen table. The clock on the wall caught his eye, its loud ticking ringing in his ears. He heard his parents' raised voices. They were arguing in the study. He felt bad about upsetting his father, appreciated his mother's sympathy, but it was his life, not theirs.

I've got to get out of here... Even if I can't go to Israel right away, it's time to move out to a place of my own, to get away from them and their fights. I'll get a job and earn the money to get to Israel on my own steam.

Then he remembered that Charlie had received a loan from the Zionist movement to go to Israel. He'd gone without his parents' agreement or help. He could do the same.

He went to bed, heard his parents still arguing in their bedroom, turned on his transistor radio to drown out their voices, and, after a long restless time, fell asleep.

He dreamt he was on trial for betraying his family. His father was the judge, his sister the prosecutor, his mother his defence counsel. They found him guilty.

The sentence: a lifetime in Australia.

No, he cried in his sleep, *No! I've got to go. Bora, save me!*

But Bora wasn't there. He was alone.

Chapter 7

1973: ALIYA – IMMIGRATION

Joe went to the Zionist office on St. Kilda Road.

He boarded a tram, climbing the wooden steps through the sliding door, then sat down in the open middle section where smoking was permitted. He lit his pipe and while puffing out fragrant rose scented smoke, observed the people around him. The smoke wafted out the window behind as the noisy vehicle moved along the tracks towards the city.

No one sitting in the tram looked Jewish. An old Aboriginal man in work clothes holding a case of tools got on and sat beside him. He looked out of place, just as Joe felt himself to be, amid all these "dinkum Aussies" with their sunburned red faces, their light eyes and hair. A young blonde woman sat across the aisle from him smoking a long filter cigarette. She was heavily made-up, with red-painted fingernails and bright red lipstick. Her blouse blew in the wind, revealing an ample bosom, and a gold cross swinging in front of her cleavage. He avoided her eyes, embarrassed by his lewd thoughts.

At the stop across from the Beth Weizman building, he got up and pulled the cord to stop the tram. He was sorry to leave the attractive woman behind, but he had to get off. The Aboriginal man got up to leave too.

Joe hopped off and crossed the busy road when the light changed. He walked past Beth Weizman, continued walking, confused, until he realized he'd gone in the wrong direction. He crossed over to the traffic divider, passing intersection after intersection, ruminating on whether he was doing the right thing, considering the momentous changes that awaited him. He noticed he was breathing heavily. He slowed down, and then sat down on a tram-stop bench.

After some hesitation, he got up, crossed the road again and walked back in the direction of Beth Weizman. He entered the building. He was walking into the stronghold of Jewish nationalism in Melbourne. The Hebrew letters, the Magen

David, the Israeli flag flying at half-mast (many had been killed the day before in a plane hijacking) meant he was in the right place.

Joe went through the glass door past the security guard and ascended the stairs.

He passed several offices until he saw the title: *Aliya, Immigration Coordinating Office - Dr. Avi Ganush.* He walked in, found the correct room, and entered.

The secretary greeted him curtly:

"You can wait here. I'll call you when Dr. Ganush is ready."

"OK. Thank you," he said, and then sat down, picked up a magazine to read.

The secretary got up and walked through a glass door that clicked closed behind her.

The magazine he held in his hand was called "Menorah" (The Lamp). It was a sports journal. Flipping through it he spotted a familiar face, looked down at the caption – Shirley Levine! A neighbour.

"You can go in now, sir."

She smiled encouragingly at him, her manicured hand pointing out the way. Her nails reminded him of the big-busted lady in the tram. Hers were the same colour. He rose, stepped in that direction, hesitantly knocked on the door.

"Come in... Come in!"

Dr. Ganush got up, shook his hand, waved him into a chair at his desk, sat opposite him on an upholstered chair. He had a long, sallow face.

"How can I help you, Mr. Kamens?"

"Joe, sir. Um... aliya... I'd like to immigrate to Israel... feel my place is there."

Dr. Ganush looked up from a paper he'd glanced at, pushed it aside, picked up a pitcher, poured two cups of water, offered one to Joe as he spoke:

"Have you been to Israel before? Any relatives, friends there?"

"Um... I was there for a summer a couple of years ago and I

know one family on a kibbutz."

The man smiled.

"Mmm... That's good, Joe. Should be of help. Which kibbutz?"

"Lochamei HaGetaot..."

"Excellent. They have an ulpan there. Who do you know?"

"The Avramis."

"Yes, I know Motti from my army days. Sad about their son... killed a few years ago... They would be a great contact for you, maybe they could be your kibbutz parents. How do you know them?"

"My mum and Rivka are friends. They were in a D.P. camp in Germany together."

Joe took a sip of water and then asked:

"Friends of mine told me you give loans to help."

"That's right. We offer a loan of three hundred dollars that becomes a grant if you stay. This is a form for you to fill in."

Joe reached over to take the papers. His hand was shaking.

"Thank you, Dr. Ganush."

"Call me Avi. And Mazel Tov (congratulations) on doing what every Jew should do!"

"By the way, Avi, do you maybe know a man called Joseph Borowski?"

Dr. Ganush abruptly put down his cup, spilling some water, before responding:

"No. Never heard the name. Why?"

After a hesitation, Joe said: "Doesn't matter. Thank you again. Bye"

He felt the man had looked at him strangely when he mentioned Bora's name... but maybe he just imagined that... He went downstairs again, out into St. Kilda Road, walked along the road away from the city centre looking for his tram stop to take him back to Caulfield. He was sweating, but it wasn't hot that day.

Joe stood at the bus stop daydreaming. He thought about visiting Rivka at her kibbutz. He imagined finding Bora, with her help, hearing about his daring past, about the wars of Israel, and he himself becoming a kibbutznik... and a soldier.

A very crowded bus drove past without stopping; another bus was not long in coming. He travelled a few stops and got off at the stop by the Carlisle Street and Hotham Street traffic lights. He passed the red brick Hassidic centre (the "Yeshiva"), and a few blocks later turned right into tree-lined Waterloo Avenue. He soon reached Adam's house, the familiar entrance way with its climbing vine.

He knocked, heard the creaking of wooden floorboards, then the door swung open.

"Joe! Hi! I've been waiting for you to come."

Adam gave him a bear hug, accompanied him from the brightly lit entrance into the kitchen.

"Tea or coffee?"

"You know the answer to that, Adam!"

"Yep. You're right. Didn't need to ask. You want a strong, black coffee."

"Right. Thank you."

Adam put the electric kettle on. It sat on a crowded marble counter, surrounded by jars and containers, filled with various kinds of tea, and spices. Joe saw some yellow saffron, turmeric, and a bright orange jar labelled green tea. He could smell the sweet odour of cloves and saw a very large jar of mustard. An exotic kitchen.

Joe looked at his old friend as he made the coffee, poured the hot water, added milk for himself, sugar for Joe. Adam had grown a beard since he'd last seen him. He looked different, more serious. He was beginning to bald, his hair receding in the middle of his hairline. His muscular hands were ruddy, and his nails dirty. The traces of oil and charcoal on both hands left marks on the counter and on the cups. Joe considered him handsome and understood why the girls were frustrated that he wasn't interested in them.

His coming out as gay was difficult for both Adam and for himself. It made him very uncomfortable. He wondered whether Adam had seen him as an object of his sexual fantasies. That left him cold.

"You're still working in the garage?"

"Yes. But I'm moving to Sydney soon. I'll be studying anthropology there. I've got to leave Melbourne now, to keep my distance from the local Jewish community."

"I understand. I'm planning to leave Melbourne soon, too."

"To Israel, right? To a kibbutz? You're following the path Dror set for you. Doing what you're supposed to do. Being a 'good boy' again!"

"Don't be so cynical! I guess you're right, but I'm choosing to do it. No one's forcing me to."

"So, what happened with the Israeli emissary, the 'aliya' man? What're your plans now?"

"He gave me a form to fill in, told me I could get some money from them. That was good news. I really needed to hear that since my parents are opposed to my going to Israel now."

"Sounds like he was helpful."

"Yes. I guess you could say that, but…"

"But what?"

"I asked him if he knew Bora. He said no, but his reaction was strange."

"You're obsessed with that, Joe. Are you still shlepping that coat around, too?"

"I'm going to find Bora over there and return the coat to him."

"Good luck with that!"

Adam laughed.

A week later, at home. A phone call...

Lily: "Here, Joe, it's for you. He said his name's Ganush."

Joe: "Hello Avi."

Lily hovered nearby until Joe waved her away, annoyed. She walked off in a huff.

"Congratulations, Joe, your loan has been confirmed. A cheque is on its way in the mail."

"Great. I'm going to the kibbutz we talked about. I'm starting ulpan there in July."

"You mentioned Bora when we met..."

"You do know him after all?" Joe took a deep breath and listened hard.

"Not exactly. I can't tell you much, but there is someone on that kibbutz who might help you in your search. His name is Gershon. Just tell him Dr. Ganush sent you."

Chapter 8
Farewell, Melbourne!

Joe's friends organized a farewell party for him the week he
left for Israel. Adam had moved to another state, Charlie
had already moved to Israel, but other old Dror friends were
there, and some of his new friends from Monash.

Judy didn't call and didn't show up.

He called her to say goodbye the next day. They talked a long
time about school days, the time in Dror, the crazy politics on
campus, the theatre Judy was involved in.

"You know, Joe. I don't understand why you're going to
Israel. There are wars over there, compulsory army service, and
a new language. And you'll have to start at a disadvantage in
a foreign country."

"I know all that, Judy, but I feel it's my duty to go. And I
want to find Bora. Remember that old coat I used to wear every
winter, the one with the bullet hole in it? I'm going to return
it to him."

"Yes. I do. You loved that coat a lot, but you stopped wearing
it this past year. I noticed that. And I think you should let go of
your obsession with this Bora of yours!"

"Well, anyway, maybe, but first... I want to talk to him about
the past."

"I'm going to miss you, Joe."

"I'll write. I promise."

"I will, too. And I'll visit you. I love you, Joe."

Joe didn't know what he felt, or what to say. He blew her
a kiss and hung up.

That evening he packed. He would wear the old partisan
coat on the trip. He had learned that winters could be cold in
the Galilee where he was first headed. Eva had repaired the
torn pocket. If he did find Bora, it would be right to return it
to him. It might make a good conversation starter about his
partisan past during the Second World War.

55

His father drove them to the airport. Joe sat beside him in the front, Eva, and Lily in the back. Yanosh turned the radio on to the classical music station. They listened to Chopin, then some Brahms. His father whistled with the music until his mother asked him to stop. The musical journey felt surreal to him, as did his family's silence, punctuated occasionally by short meaningless interchanges.

They entered the airport building, delivered his things to check-in, and found a table to sit at while they waited for the flight to be announced. His father brought drinks and they sipped as they made their last comments.

"Rivka will take good care of you."

"I know Mum. I know."

"You're taking that old fur coat with you?"

"Yes."

"Well, you can give it back to Bora when you catch up with him. Buy yourself something better."

"I will Dad."

"Judy asked me to kiss you goodbye, for her too, Joey."

"That's it. Time to go. They just announced my flight!"

They each hugged and kissed him in turn. Joe squirmed as his sister kissed him twice. He was smiling from ear to ear as he walked away. He turned back to look through the glass partition. He saw his sister waving goodbye, his parents standing sombrely by, their arms linked. Lily and his mother were crying, his dad looked stoic. Joe waved a final goodbye to them. He didn't know how long it would be until he might see them again.

Joe turned and strode away.

Part 2
ISRAEL

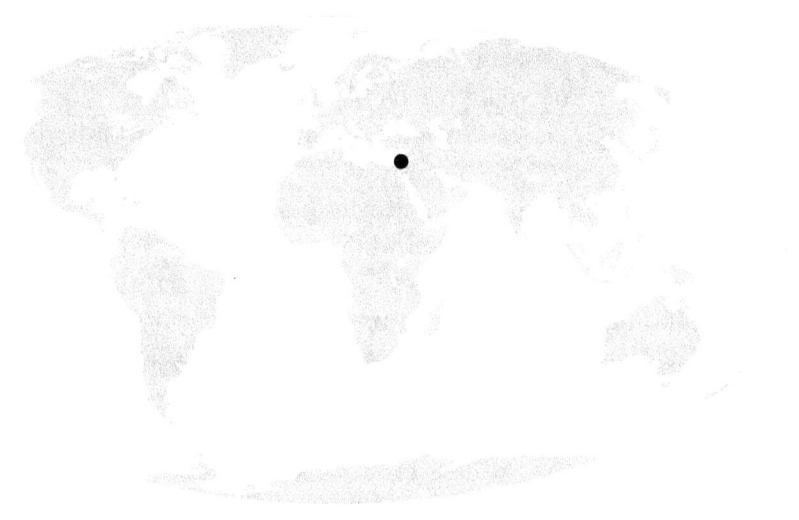

Chapter 9

LOCHAMEI HAGETAOT, THE GHETTO FIGHTERS KIBBUTZ

Joe sat at the Pesach Seder table in the kibbutz, reflecting on his memories of the festival of freedom. He looked at the old, worn faces of the kibbutz members sitting near him; he saw the fire in Rivka's eyes. She sat next to him explaining what was happening. He remembered the Seder ritual meal in the youth movement in Melbourne. They called it "the third Seder" as there were two in most family homes before that, but for him it was special, the most important Seder... the one that mattered, some years it was his only one.

He imagined that Rivka, who had told him about her youth movement days in Warsaw with such enthusiasm and love, must have had similar memories herself. This Seder in Kibbutz Lochamei HaGetaot reminded him of that youth movement milieu. It had a similar feel to it, but also a sad undertone that weighed on the festivities of this "festival of freedom". The recent European past? The multitude of lost family members? The heavy cost of survival and building a new country? The room was full of heavy memories...

Bora too was in the air, or at least his spirit was. Joe heard his name mentioned repeatedly. Rivka lit up at the sound of his name. He remembered a story his parents had told him about a dramatic Seder at a D.P. camp in Germany, disrupted by an attempt to assassinate Bora.

A children's choir led the community in song, the elders joined in the singing in heavily accented Hebrew. Then a white-haired man took the microphone to begin the proceedings with a few words from a prepared text, but he had trouble getting everyone's attention. It was very noisy.

Joe remembered third Seders at the moadon in Melbourne, the long trestle tables laid out with white tablecloths, adorned with flowers, the posters on the walls of early halutzim (pioneers) working the fields of the Land. He remembered the joyful singing, the Israeli dances, the celebration of spring. He looked around the kibbutz dining hall: the walls were decorated with paintings of fields of grain before harvest, of boys and girls in white tunics, dancing hair with garlands of red and purple flowers. These middle-aged people were actual halutzim – sitting around him at the tables, arguing about the food, the program, the work schedules, the Party and the Party leadership, and about other prosaic economic issues.

In Dror, he had felt a certain spirituality, or, at least, a spirit... the spirit of youth. On this kibbutz it was different, not what he had expected. These tired, worn faces belied spirituality; these people were sad, their youthful joy and enthusiasm long gone. The younger kibbutz members, called the "sabras", had a cynical look in their eyes, they were smiling, almost laughing at the idealistic speeches. He heard some mumbled negative comments; saw their impatience with the old Zionist cliches.

The Seder narrative unfolded from the children singing "*Ma Nishtana* – Why is this night different than all other nights". In his Melbourne parental home, the retelling was dominated by Holocaust memories, and a sense of profound loss.

The Pesach feast on the kibbutz reminded him of his parents' and their friends' Seders much more than the livelier youth movement version. In Dror, they did not talk about the war and the Nazis all the time but here they did, just like his parents and their friends had. In one sense, he felt at home amongst these people, but in another, he felt like a stranger, felt he was a young outsider who could not participate fully. He followed some of the Hebrew and even some Yiddish but... there were allusions, associations that he didn't understand. These survivors, like his parents and their friends, were remnants of another reality, human fragments of an obliterated world.

The Pesach Holiday ended.

Joe settled into a routine, learning Hebrew in the kibbutz ulpan during the mornings, working in their plastics factory in the afternoons. He enjoyed the Hebrew studies but found the work in the factory boring.

He made a point of visiting Rivka and Motti a couple of afternoons each week after work. Rivka was warm and welcoming, Motti gruff but friendly.

A couple of weeks after Pesach, as the weather warmed with the approach of a first hamsin (desert heat wave), Joe invited Nancy, a fellow ulpan student he was interested in, to come visit his "adopted kibbutz family." They walked down a flower-lined stone path from the communal dining hall to the "schoonat vatikim" (veterans' quarter), reaching Rivka's herb garden to find her sitting under a carob tree on a deck chair, reading a newspaper. That day another soldier had been killed in the north.

Dry leaves under their feet crackled as they approached. Rivka looked up at them red-eyed.

"Hello, Yossi."

She tried to smile but Joe could see she was in pain. He knew why.

"Um... maybe we should come some other time, Rivka?"

"Yes, I'd appreciate that."

They left for a walk along the beach as Joe told Nancy about Oded. Nancy was sweet, holding his hand as she listened. They kissed. They started doing their homework together, sharing stories about their childhood, visited Rivka and Motti together after work a few times.

When the ulpan studies ended, the young students moved on to other kibbutzim, to the cities or went back to America, France, or England. Nancy, too, left. She went back to Milwaukee to start college. They promised to write to each other and parted as friends.

"I'll be living somewhere else by the time I write to you." Joe told her.

"You're not going to stay here?" Nancy asked.

"No. I have to move on."

He explained that he could not stay on this old kibbutz any longer, he felt that his presence was awkward. He was constantly aware of Rivka and Motti's loss of their son. It burdened him to think she was comparing him to her lost baby, relating to him as compensation for that loss.

After Nancy's departure, Joe corresponded with his parents about his plans, explained that he needed a change. They asked him to come home to Melbourne. They would pay the fare back. His answer to that on the phone was:

"Not yet, Mum. I haven't found Bora here, just a few memories of him from Rivka and from a man called Gershon. But I'll find him. I'm still searching."

"Joe, I think you're wasting your time," was the answer.

The partisan coat was a constant reminder that he had a mission yet to accomplish. After he had returned it to its partisan owner, he'd be able to leave the Holocaust and its haunting stories behind, to get away from the irksome burden of that past.

Joe remembered his Canadian friend, Steve Goland. Steve had invited him to come to his kibbutz. It was a younger, newer, kibbutz on the Golan Heights, called "Afikei Kinneret".

He remembered meeting Steve in the Arab market in the old city of Jerusalem, on his previous 1970 visit to Israel. He liked Steve, found him interesting to talk to. They had a great time diving together in Eilat and remained in contact afterwards across continents through their letters.

Not long before leaving Australia for Israel, Joe received a letter from Steve. Steve had returned to Israel from his native Toronto and was now living on Afikei Kinneret. He described his life on the new kibbutz.

Joe wrote to Steve telling him of his aliya decision. Steve wrote back:

"Joe, it would be great if you came! This young kibbutz needs volunteers willing to work and it's an opportunity to get involved at an important early stage in the community's development. I think you should consider joining me here as a volunteer. I'm willing to speak to the people in charge, if you're interested."

At the time, Joe wasn't sure, answered him in a vague fashion. He didn't like the idea of joining a settlement beyond the green line. He thought it was a problem to settle civilians in an area conquered in war, an area under dispute. He didn't write that to his friend. He just wrote:

"I have family friends at another kibbutz willing to help me. They have an ulpan. It's a more central place. I want to try that first, and then we'll see. I'll call you when I'm in the country."

But in the excitement of first coming to the country, learning the new language, his relationship with Nancy, and his frustrating search for Bora (all roads led nowhere!), he neglected his friend Steve. Now, he remembered him.

He searched his rucksack and found the notebook in which he'd scribbled phone numbers for his trip to Israel. He flipped through the pages until he found Steve's scribbled number. He dialed it...

"Hello, Joe!"

"Steve, how are you? I promised to call. I'm back in Israel!"

"Great to hear your voice, Joe. How long have you been in the country?"

"I'm, ah...actually I've been in Israel since December," he admitted.

"Oh, really. That long? And you didn't contact or phone all this time?"

"Well, I... uh... have been staying on Kibbutz Lochamei HaGetaot. The truth is I want to get out of here. I've had an overdose of Holocaust survivors, and their traumatic memories."

"Yeah, I get that. No one that old here. When're you coming?"

"Um...gimme a couple of days to say my goodbyes and then I'll head out. How do I get there?"

"Ah... yeah. It isn't that easy. There are just two buses a day. A kibbutz driver goes down to Tiberias once a day... delivery trucks sometimes come up. You can hitch a ride from Tzemach intersection."

"Wow. Sounds like a problem getting to you. I guess you're kind of isolated up there."

"You could say that, yes. It's isolated. A kibbutz driver picks people up sometimes on the way back from Tiberias... I'll find out when that is, whether there's room, and get back to you. How do I contact you?"

"Ah... I don't have a phone, but you can call the kibbutz office and leave a message with Rivka – everyone here knows her."

"OK. I'll do that. Do you have warm clothes? It gets cold up here in the Golan in winter."

"Sure. I've got a fur coat. It has a story to it. I'll tell you all about it when I come."

The next day, when he visited Rivka in her small kibbutz apartment, he found her busy sorting old letters.

He noticed she had been crying.

"Is there something the matter, Rivka?"

"Just looking at old letters from my Warsaw friends."

"Oh."

"None of them survived the war…"

"I have something to tell you..." Joe started saying to her, knowing that continuing talking about the past in Poland would make it difficult to talk about anything else.

She looked up at him expectantly.

"Oh, yes... Good news? A new girlfriend? A letter from your parents?"

"No. Nothing like that. It's just that I've really appreciated your hospitality since arriving in the country. You and Motti have been generous but…"

"Let me guess. You want to start 'doing your own thing' as young people say, no?"

"Yes. That's right, Rivka. I have a friend on another kibbutz. Afikei Kinneret, a new kibbutz in Golan Heights. They need young volunteers. I've been working with Nahum in the fishponds for six weeks now and don't meet many other people. He's a nice man, but there's no one my age working with us."

Rivka smiled sadly, studied Joe for a moment, looking into his eyes with a serious expression on her face, and then said:

"Joe... I hear you. You're Eva's son, but you're also Yanosh's. You have some of your father's restlessness. You've been hearing too much about our past in Europe, our terrible losses.

63

I understand. My Oded didn't want to hear about the past anymore either... before he went to the army..."

Her voice was strained.

"I understand," she repeated, choking back emotion.

"But, Rivka, what you and your friends have done here is incredible after what you went through."

Joe hugged her.

"What is this? A goodbye? I expect you to stay in contact! You're like a son to us now. I promised your mother I'd help you in any way I could..."

"I know. I know. Of course, I'll still visit and keep you updated, but maybe that too is a reason why I need to move on."

The front door opened and slammed shut again. Rivka's husband, Motti, walked in filling the entrance to the room with his great bulk. He was wearing blue overalls and had a big grin on his face.

He walked past them, holding up a large dark hand stained with grease and oil. He soon came back and sat down with them, turned to Joe, and asked:

"So how are you, chaver... my young friend?"

"He just told me he's leaving us. Going to a different kibbutz."

"Is that so Joe? You aren't happy here? What's the story?"

Joe nodded.

He liked Motti, despite his gruff manner. He didn't often say much but his presence gave people a feeling of strength. And safety. It was strange that a war invalid – he'd lost his hand to a grenade in the War of Independence – was able to do that, but that was what Joe felt when with him. He'd heard from others on the kibbutz that Motti was much respected, had been something of a hero, had saved lives in battle.

Joe saw that Rivka and Motti were a loving couple, doted on each other. He sometimes felt like an intruder in their snug love nest. He wished his parents had been more like them.

"Joe, let me give you a word of advice," Motti said, looking serious and concerned.

"When you get to your new place next week, go for a walk. Check it out. Look at how they keep their gardens and public spaces. Go to the dining hall and look for the work roster. Study it to see who's who, who works where and who is in charge in each workplace. Find out who's the boss. Check out their announcements of cultural activities. Check their roster for rides in and out of the kibbutz and learn who the drivers are."

"Wow, Motti that's a lot of advice. A lot of homework to do right away... why? Are you that suspicious of another kibbutz?"

"Because you don't want to commit yourself to a place that's not well run or to a kibbutz that's run by a small clique of self-interested people to whom you are just cheap labour. You'll quickly see if the gardens or the public spaces are divided between an "in" and an "out" group or not, and whether there's a closed elitist culture, or a more open one. If they are elitist, then get out of there right away, or you'll suffer."

Joe stared at him, astonished at his pedantic outburst. Rivka looked annoyed at her husband.

"Mordechai! What are you telling him!? All places have elites, they don't function otherwise. Lochamei HaGetaot is no different than any other kibbutz in that respect."

"That's true... but there are more selfish and less selfish elites; there are closed, secretive ones and open, nurturing ones. Here people are invited to participate, are treated with respect, efforts are made to include new people, to share information and encourage involvement. That's not true in all places. Some of those young settlers, so called "pioneers", who have settled in the new territories aren't open or inclusive. Joe, just be careful, and remember you have a home here with us."

"I agree with that. Of course, Motti. But I think Joe will have to learn and find out such things for himself. After he leaves, he'll appreciate our community here more, I'm sure... but now..."

She started crying, wiped her tears away, and then fell silent. Motti place his arm around her shoulder.

Joe just nodded. He was thinking to himself: *"They are being overprotective, like my parents."*

He finished his coffee, got up to go and gave each of his kibbutz "parents" a hug before leaving.

"I'll be back the day after tomorrow to say goodbye," he told them.

"And think about my words of advice!"

"OK, I will."

He closed the screen door behind him and walked along the path back to his room. He noticed that the bushes and flower beds on the way were all the same. Pretty, well-kept and repeating themselves: block after block of acacia bushes interspersed with yellow and red roses. Their socialist standardization could be seen in their gardening, each garden the same as the next. He remembered a popular American satirical song "Little boxes, little boxes... all made of ticky tacky..."

Chapter 10
An Aussie Friend Visits, Meeting with Gershon

One of the only gardens that was different was Rivka's. She had planted unusual shrubs, some cactuses, and had a patch in which she grew her own herbs. And a carob tree shaded it all. When, some afternoons after work, he would sit with them in Rivka's garden under the tree, he would enjoy the special fragrances of those herbs.

He looked back along the path again, hoping to see once more the brightly coloured array below Motti and Rivka's veranda. It was already out of sight.

I will remember that garden when I'm far away...

Joe reached his room in the "Ravakia", the singles' quarter. He kicked off his shoes, walked across the wooden floor, strewn with empty beer bottles and dirty plastic cups, and shoved the newspapers and magazines off his bed. He poured himself a cup of beer and sat down to relax. He reached for the 'Jerusalem Post' lying on the floor beside his woollen tartan slippers. A headline caught his eye: "Negotiations – Israelis and Egyptians meet at 100-kilometer checkpoint"; below it a picture of generals standing next to a tent. He recognized Ariel Sharon, began to read.

Someone knocked on the door. Three loud knocks.

"Who's there?!" he called out, annoyed at the intrusion.

"It is I!" a familiar voice responded as the door opened. A ruddy hand coming out of a green pullover sleeve was holding the doorknob.

Joe watched in disbelief as Adam stepped into the room. He looked different, strange.

"Adam! Where did you come from? What are you doing here in Israel?"

Looking at his old childhood friend more closely, he was shocked at what he saw.

Adam had put on a lot of weight. He was shaven, completely shaven – no beard, no hair on his head, no eyebrows, and the top of his chest that showed through the v-cut in his pullover had also been shaved.

"I thought I'd drop by to visit an old friend!"

Adam put down a brown duffle bag and held out his arms to hug Joe who had meanwhile got himself up to greet him. They hugged. Joe offered Adam his folding chair, kicking newspapers out of the way to make room for it.

"Have a seat. Best I can do," he said, laughing. "Here, let me pour you some beer, too. So, what's new, Adam?"

"Just arrived from Ireland. Spent time in Belfast and Dublin. Very interesting and complicated situation they have over there. A friend I studied with invited me. Anyway, I thought I'd just pop in and catch up with you on my way back to Australia. How are ya', Joe? You're looking good. Suntanned! And you've developed some muscle. They're working you hard here on this kibbutz?"

"I guess you can say that. I'm working in the fishponds. That's in the sun, and it's vigorous work. But, Adam, how did you know to find me here!? We haven't been in contact in quite a while, maybe a year now."

"Oh, I know, but that was easy. When I got back to Melbourne from Sydney after I finished my final exams I asked after you. People told me you were living on some kibbutz. So, I called Judy. I was sure she would know where you were. She did."

"Yeah. I've been corresponding with her since I left the country. I invited her to join me here, but she had other plans. Anyway, that was smart of you to track me down like that, but why didn't you write, instead of just showing up like this? I mightn't have been here."

"Don't know. Just wanted to surprise you. Anyway, Judy told me you'd finished your degree and had done very well at uni, but that instead of continuing, as they invited you to do, you just got up and left. Why? What happened?"

"Yom Kippur War. So many guys our age died. I felt it was time to come to Israel, to help, to replace the boys who fell. And then while I was mulling these things, Charlie just dropped everything and went. So, I decided to go too."

"I heard about Charlie. Crazy. But I thought he was a leftist, critical of Israel and how it treats the Arabs. He was born in Israel. He must have known they would take him to the army when he came; but he went anyway."

"You know he's in the army now?"

"Yep. I plan to visit him while I'm here," Adam said, smiling.

"That's not so easy to do. I visited him while he was in basic training a couple of times. He'd lost a lot of weight and didn't look great. Kind of depressed, I think. He was in an army base near here before, near Pardes Hana, but I've lost contact now. Don't know where he is."

"Oh. Sounds worrying." Adam's smile was gone.

Joe nodded, then looked at his watch.

"Umm. It's getting to be dinner time. Come with me to the dining hall. And let's talk on the way. Just leave your stuff here. Maybe Rivka and Motti will be there. I can introduce you to them and I'm sure they can help arrange things so you can stay a day or two. I'm planning to move on to another kibbutz next week."

"To where?"

"The Golan Heights. I have a friend who's invited me there. It's a new kibbutz."

"Mmm... Maybe I can try out kibbutz life for a while myself... umm... Who are Rivka and Motti?"

"My kibbutz parents. I'll explain, but let's go!"

They walked out the door together. It banged shut behind them, the torn mosquito screen swinging back and forth.

They walked out through a row of bushes and along the dirt path, Joe telling Adam about life on the kibbutz and his pioneering plans. Adam listened.

They reached the dining hall. The clatter of cups, plates, cutlery, and the chatter of people greeted them as they passed the cluttered notice board, entered through the big wooden double doors, and waded into a flood of noise and lights, and moving kibbutz members carrying trays.

Joe told Adam that they had heard of Bora here on the kibbutz, that there was a kibbutz member, Gershon Ben Ami, who had been with him in Germany after the Second World War. Bora and Gershon had been involved in the "Avengers".

"That's interesting, Joe. What's the Avengers?"

"A bunch of ex-partisans like Bora who knocked off Nazis after the war."

"Wow! I'd like to hear more about that. Can we find this Gershon and ask him questions?"

"Sure, that's just what I plan to do here."

"Do you still wear Bora's old coat with the bullet hole in it?"

"Yes."

"I still remember that you used to make up stories about that coat and where it had been during the war."

Joe led Adam to a long white building with a row of aluminium-framed windows.

"Umm, we will look for Gershon here. He always eats dinner in the "hadar ochel". He usually sits alone by the far window."

"I remember that word from our youth movement days... hadar ochel."

"That's right. It means dining hall."

They waited in the queue, took trays and loaded them with cucumber and tomato salad, eggs, bread, and some cheese.

"A typical kibbutz supper," Joe explained. "The breakfasts are the same."

They manoeuvred around the tables as Joe searched for Motti and Rivka, passing a table of rowdy American volunteers who laughingly greeted Joe with "G'day, mate!" He waved but kept walking. He couldn't see his kibbutz parents anywhere. But he did see Gershon in his usual spot, by the window on the far side of the hall, studying the people in the room, smoking his pipe (or was he just sucking on it? – there wasn't any smoke coming out of it). Joe saw a cup of black tea steaming in front of him, the usual cube of sugar on the saucer beside it.

Gershon was short and stocky, his feet barely reaching the floor. He had a massive head of white curly hair and a closely shaven face full of deeply etched lines and wrinkles. Adam whispered to Joe that the man looked like an aging boxer or wrestler. One of his ears was misshapen, as if someone had ripped or bitten off a piece of it, leaving a long-jagged scar along the bottom instead of an earlobe.

"Can we join you, Gershon?"

The man grunted a reluctant agreement. They sat down opposite him, laying down their plastic trays and organizing their food in front of them. Adam went back to fetch hot drinks, leaving Joe and Gershon alone.

"Who is your friend, Joe?... Another Australian?"

"Yes. He was in the same youth movement. Remember, I told you about Dror."

Gershon had learned his Yiddish-accented English in a British internment camp.

"I told my friend, Adam, about the Avengers, about your "work" in Germany after the Second World War. I'd like to hear more. But let's wait until Adam comes back."

Gershon nodded and turned his head to the window. Joe followed the direction of Gershon's gaze and saw a pair of cooing yellow-beaked black birds necking on the branch of the large eucalyptus tree opposite the open window.

"A loving couple," Gershon said, wistfully.

Joe realized that he knew nothing about Gershon's personal life. Had he ever married? Did he have children? He always sat there alone by the window, smoking his pipe, looking outside, ignoring the other kibbutz members and the volunteers.

"They were killed by the Germans," Gershon said, in answer to the unasked question.

He sounded matter of fact, emotionless, his voice almost metallic.

"They?"

"My wife, Sonia, and my son, Yonatan..."

"I'm sorry. I didn't know..."

"That's because I never talk about it. It's the past. I had to move on with life... after it all ended."

He winked at Joe as Adam approached, carrying a small tray with two cups, spoons, and little packets of sugar.

71

"So, you two want to know more about the Avengers?"
Adam nodded.

"Yes, how did the group evolve after the war?" Joe asked.

"Well... it was after I realized the full extent of the Nazi mass murder, after I understood what those pigs, *yamach shemam* (curse them), had done, that they had systematically slaughtered six million Jews. When we came out of the forests in 1944, the war wasn't over. As we came to town after town, then cities, crossed borders, and found no Jews, started hearing about the camps, the trains, the gas, we began to understand the immensity of the Nazi crime. It was unbelievable. The Jews everywhere were gone – all gone, wiped out, as if they'd never existed."

"We know all that," Adam commented dryly.

"I had wanted revenge during the war. I found my way to the forest in Rudniki, joined the partisans there, and met a strange, haunted man, named Abba Kovner. We were all haunted, but he was different, he was obsessed. He was from Vilna, had been a leader of the underground in the ghetto. He was already a known Yiddish poet."

"Yes. I've heard of him," Joe interjected.

"After the war I met him in Bucharest. We all wanted to get to Palestine. He told us that he had an idea, a plan for revenge after the war ended. He said that it was not enough to kill a few German S.S. men. What they had done required something bigger – in Germany itself."

"So that was how the Avengers came into being. It was Kovner's idea. Was that how you met Joseph Borowski?"

"I told you about that, Joe."

"Yes, but Adam here wants to hear about it too."

Adam nodded.

Joe's coffee was cold. He hadn't touched it while listening to Gershon.

Adam was still sipping his tea. He stopped when Bora was mentioned.

"Everyone in that crowd knew Bora. He'd made a name for himself as a partisan leader. He derailed thirty-two German trains, had a Gestapo price on his head and had saved the lives of two hundred other Jews who had reached the Naroch forest."

"OK, Bora was a war hero but what did he have to do with what went on after the war?" Adam asked.

"I'm getting to that. A little patience please... Abba sought him out. They met first in Vilna, then in Bialystok."

Across the hall, Joe saw Rivka just leaving the hadar ochel with friends, but she left before he could wave to get her attention. He didn't want to miss a word of what he was hearing. Adam didn't notice.

Gershon continued speaking: "There was a Jewish historical commission set up, they collected testimonies of Nazi atrocities. Bora came to give testimony and that's where Kovner caught up with him. Bora agreed to make his way to Germany to help him organize revenge on a grander scale."

"What do you mean by... 'a grander scale'?" Joe asked, rubbing the stubble on his chin.

"Kovner planned to kill six million Germans, one for each Jew murdered. He wanted an act of Biblical dimensions that would deter antisemites in future."

Joe stared at Gershon, too shocked to speak.

"What! I don't believe what I'm hearing. The man must have been mad!" Adam exclaimed.

"Those were different times... Kovner was passionate. He told us Palestine can wait, that we had to act right away before more Jews were slaughtered by another madman. He had Stalin in mind."

Joe looked over at Adam. They'd never heard this story before from either of their parents in Melbourne.

Gershon smiled to himself, continued puffing his pipe, then turned his gaze outside, his eyes seemed glazed. Joe's eyes followed his gaze out the window. Birds singing in a tree nearby caught his ear. He saw children playing peacefully on the kibbutz lawn. He could see nothing unusual out there. The man's eyes were somewhere else far away, his look caused Joe to shudder before asking:

"And? Go on…" Adam was shifting his position on his plastic

seat, now sitting forward. Joe straightened his posture, listened intently to Gershon as he spoke.

"We reached Germany, organized secret cells of avengers. Kovner left for Palestine to win the support of the Zionist leadership. We waited weeks without a word until the news reached us that he was arrested by the British on his way back with poison. They found nothing on him. He'd thrown the poison overboard. After that, we lowered our sights. Some left for Palestine, had doubts about the whole crazy plan. Without his leadership, enthusiasm died. Those of us left decided to focus on the actual murderers – the S.S. henchmen."

"How many did you kill?" asked Adam.

"Not enough. The British and the Americans started looking for us, and things were getting hot in Palestine at the time, so we had to close the operation."

"And then what?"

"Then most of us headed for Palestine to get ready for the coming war with the Arabs; others, like Bora, continued their war against the Nazis."

"Is that why Bora came to Australia?" Adam asked Gershon.

"Yes, he was chasing an S.S. man called Schultz. He found the bastard and took care of him."

Gershon lifted his hand to his throat, pulled a finger across it in a cutting motion, and winked at Joe and Adam.

He continued:

"Erwin Schultz was one of the organizers of the "Odessa", a clandestine organization of ex-S.S. men, set up to help them escape justice, to smuggle Nazi war criminals out of Europe to safe havens. Some went to Arab countries, others, like Adolf Eichmann, headed for South America. Schultz had a brother in Sydney."

"Ah, so that's the Australian connection?!" Joe exclaimed.

"Yes. After that Bora had to lay low for a while until he could return to Eretz Israel to join our fight for independence."

"He lived in Melbourne for a while?" Joe asked, surprised.

"Yes. He had to hide out after the assassination at first. Later he was useful there as an undercover agent. Schultz wasn't the only war criminal in Australia."

"But why was this Nazi so important that they sent someone all the way to Australia?" Adam asked.

"Erwin Schultz was a commander of an Einzatsgruppen killing squad, responsible for the murder of hundreds of thousands of Jews in Belarus, including Bora's family, but never brought to trial at Nuremberg. He escaped a prison camp for S.S. men and disappeared until we heard from the Australian survivors."

"I think they're closing the hadar ochel now. They're flicking lights on and off hinting that."

"Don't worry. They do that for a while, most people leave, then they stop."

"Yeah, but we're in the way. The toranim – the cleaning crew – want to wipe down the tables."

Gershon smiled at the two young men.

"Would you two like to come to my room?"

"Thanks, Gershon, but Adam just arrived," Joe said. "I want to set him up for the night. Could we meet you in the moadon haverim after that?"

"Yes. I could meet you there, about 8:00 p.m."

Gershon had a strange glassy-eyed look. Later, thinking back, Joe realized that something was wrong.

Joe and Adam got up, brought their trays and plates to the dishwashers, while the lights continued flicking on and off.

"See you later, Gershon."

"Nice to meet you. See you."

Gershon relit his pipe and remained sitting alone by the window watching them, and everyone else, leave the dining hall. He was sitting in a darkened part of the hall at last glance back at him, the light of the pipe shining in the gloom.

Joe settled Adam in a room, then led him to the moadon. Gershon didn't show up. They asked around. No one had seen him, no one knew where he was. After they had a couple of drinks and an hour had passed, they went to bed, wondering what had become of him.

The next morning Gershon was the talk of the kibbutz. He was found dead in his room. The police came, and a physician, to examine the body. No note was left, and no one could testify to any reason why he might have taken his own life. It wasn't clear whether it was an overdose or suicide. Some pills were found on the floor by the bed, and an empty bottle labelled as a migraine medication.

"Pretty strong stuff!" the police doctor had commented before he left.

Joe was stunned by all this, as were most people on the kibbutz. Motti and Rivka were less surprised. Motti said that Gershon was a weird guy who kept to himself and had few friends, that he always looked unhappy.

Joe and Adam attended the funeral. It was a quiet, modest affair. Many kibbutz members did their duty and came, but there was no religious ceremony, and little was said. Shlomo Lahat, mayor of Tel Aviv, showed up. According to Motti, there were also a couple of Mossad secret service agents there. They each laid a stone on the grave and left. Joe was surprised that no one said the mourner's Kaddish prayer either. He hoped that Bora would make an appearance, but he didn't.

Chapter 11
THE ACCIDENT, A NEW KIBBUTZ

December 1974. Winter. A fine drizzle, everything was damp, the leaves on the nearby trees glistened with tiny drops, the rough road was spotted with puddles in potholes. Joe and Adam stood on the corner, shivering, and huddled in their now wet clothes, waiting for the ride. A grey and battered van pulled over to pick them up at the Tzemach junction. The sliding door, dented in places, newly painted in others, rolled open. Joe saw it was full of young people: two sat in the very back seat, two in the middle, and gripping the steering wheel sat a dour-looking driver, unshaven with dark circles under his eyes. Sitting beside him was a big woman loaded with shopping bags.

Joe was wearing his partisan coat. He worried that its thickness and bulk might make a problem when squeezing himself into the van with the others.

"Where to?" the driver asked.

"The southernmost settlement up there, Afikei Kinneret," said Joe, pointing up into the hills.

"You're coming up to our kibbutz, to Afikei Kinneret?"

"Yes. We called. They said you'd be passing by here this afternoon. We've been waiting here a long time."

"I'm Joe, this is Adam."

"OK. We'll manage... You, move into the back to make room for these guys," he commanded, pointing at a girl wearing large silver earrings who looked about sixteen, not more, sitting near the door. She hopped into the back.

"I'm Shimon, the kibbutz driver. "Toss those things into the back and get in, it's getting late."

Adam and Joe threw their bags into the baggage compartment, Joe peeled off and rolled the bulky coat, then threw it in, and he and Adam slid into the middle seat.

It was uncomfortable, crowded. The other passengers glanced at them silently, each returning to their own musings.

Joe was grateful to be in the dry van, and no longer waiting for a ride in the damp outside. The door slid closed with a bang, and they started moving. They passed rows upon rows of tropical-looking trees on their left.

"What are those?" Adam asked the long-haired, one-ear-ringed young man next to him.

"Those are Kibbutz Maagan's banana trees. I worked there before moving up to Afikei Kinneret," he said in his heavy Scottish accent.

"How long have you been there?" Joe asked.

"Six months now. Nice place."

Everyone else remained silent. Adam managed a smile, Joe a friendly nod, but neither spoke further.

Shimon clicked on the car radio. Hebrew songs, and babble, interrupted by a news flash. Joe understood the gist of it: another interchange of artillery fire in the northern Golan Heights, no casualties. Shimon turned off the radio, mumbled a few words that Joe couldn't hear. Quiet was restored.

Joe looked around him. Apart from the long-haired Scotsman beside him, and Adam on his other side, three girls (the one with the silver earrings, another with blond braids and a third wrapped in a green scarf) sat behind. He'd heard them speaking English when they got in, but they'd stopped talking when he and Adam settled in.

Beside the morose driver sat an older woman adjusting her lipstick in a small mirror. The scent of her perfume filled the cabin, her bright green and purple dress spread over the remaining seat space.

Going up towards the Heights, the shimmering lake waters winked at them from between the trees. They swung around a bend in the road, leaving behind the better surfaced road around the Sea of Galilee, which was now out of sight. The drizzle had stopped, the road here was dry.

The van rolled around curves, momentarily dipping then climbing steep ascents. As they turned sharp corners going up, the passengers were thrown from one side to the other inside the van.

Suddenly, a tractor came flying around a hairpin turn in the road above them. Attached to it was a wagon with three screaming people in it. Joe watched in shock as the tractor missed the turn, flew over the road, and careened down the mountainside and overturned. The girls behind him shrieked. Everyone grabbed what they could to steady themselves as the tractor flew past them. They lunged forward as the driver braked, screeching to a halt on the side of the road. Shimon started yelling into a walkie-talkie, as everyone shakily got out of the vehicle.

Joe felt dizzy standing outside, in the sudden mayhem.

"Come quick, Shmulik!" Shimon was shouting into the instrument. "There's been an accident here on the snake path coming up from Tzemach. Call the police! An ambulance! The army! Yes, that's right, an accident! Get help. Move it! Move it. Now!"

Below, Joe could see the overturned tractor, its big back wheels still turning in the air.

Black smoke was rising from the motor as a man rolled out onto the rocky mountainside. Joe could smell the petrol fumes. There was an explosion. More, thicker, black smoke, red flames in the middle of it rose from where the tractor's engine had been.

"Oh, my God!"

"No one could survive that! They must all be dead," one of the girls said, crying.

No one else said anything. Silence, other than the sound of burning coming from below.

Shimon ran down the hill, followed by Adam. Joe froze in his tracks, just below the four women who were also frozen with fear and shock.

He heard, and then saw, a helicopter that appeared from nowhere, whirring above them, hovering above the overturned tractor. A hose emerged from a side of the helicopter and its nozzle sprayed a foamy liquid down into the fire from above, dowsing the flames until they were no more, only steamy smoke. The helicopter landed in a nearby field of thorns, its blades churning the air as soldiers leapted out and ran over to the scene of the accident.

A jeep came screeching down the hill, siren sounding. Joe heard sirens below them. An ambulance arrived from down the road, followed by a police car.

He watched in disbelief as the four soldiers who had jumped out of the helicopter pulled three mangled, blackened bodies out of the smoking twisted wreckage of the wagon.

Two medics and the ambulance driver came running down the hill carrying stretchers and medical equipment. It was too late for the passengers of the wagon. No one else was visible.

The police arrived and cordoned off the road.

Shimon and Adam stood below, near the helicopter. Joe saw they were prevented from coming too close. He watched as a man extricated himself, with help, from nearby thorns and rocks. He was the sole survivor.

The man was bleeding badly from his right arm and from the back of his head. The medics cleaned the wounds, set up a transfusion stand and bandaged him. They opened out a stretcher and lifted him onto it, one carrying the bag of transfusion fluids along beside him, as they walked back up the hill. Shimon followed the stretcher, talking to the man as they went. Adam rejoined Joe. His boots were muddy.

"What happened, Adam?"

"You didn't see!? Why didn't you come down to help too?"

"I... uh... froze. Anyway, there wasn't much I could do."

"I suppose you're right. I couldn't do anything down there either. Anyway, there were three volunteers in the wagon being pulled by that tractor. They were all killed, probably instantaneously. The driver managed to get out in time, but he is beat up bad."

"Yeah, I saw that."

"His name is Dani. He is a friend of Shimon's."

Adam showed him a bunch of keys on a ring.

"Shimon gave me these keys to the van. He asked me if I can drive. I agreed to, but it's better you drive, Joe. I'm not used to driving on the right. He told me to drive everyone up to the kibbutz. He's going with his friend to hospital in the ambulance."

Below them the helicopter was taking off, having loaded the three blanket-wrapped bodies into the craft.

Two policemen strode up the hill towards them.

"Terrible tragedy," one officer said.

"Identity papers, please," the other requested.

Each in turn presented their driving licenses, passports, or blue identity cards to the policeman.

"We would like to ask each of you a few questions as witnesses to what happened here."

After each of them, one by one, had described what they'd seen, they were ordered to come down to the police station in Tiberias the next day. The officer left. Each stood there dazed, holding their written order to report for questioning.

The police removed the barriers.

Joe started the engine, got the feel of the van, adjusted the mirrors, and started driving up the hill again. He drove cautiously up the snake path. Everyone sat silent.

They arrived at Kibbutz Afikei Kinneret before dark. As they drove in, Joe saw a row of grey concrete blocks and a few trees. Beyond them in the valley below he could see distant lights. One lonely tractor was parked in the parking lot, next to the biggest building, a wooden wagon hitched to it.

A worried woman in blue appeared, hugged the older woman, and then started bombarding them with questions.

"What happened? Where's Shimon?"

"Who are you?" she asked suddenly, looking at Joe and Adam, but before they, or anyone else, could respond, she continued: "I'm Selma, the kibbutz secretary. You're traumatized by the accident, I'm sure. It's dinner time. Follow me. Everyone is waiting inside to hear what happened."

She led them into the dining hall, announced their arrival, waited for quiet and read a phone message they had just received from Shimon.

"Shimon is with Dani in the hospital. He lost a lot of blood, has multiple fractures and a concussion, but he'll live. About the three killed, you all know. We'll inform the families, of course, when we know details of the funerals. Please don't overwhelm the newcomers with questions. Let's all eat now."

Everyone started talking at once, peppering the arrivals with questions. No one sat down to eat.

Joe recognized Steve in the concerned crowd waiting. He was tall and lanky, so tall that he would stand out in any crowd. He came up to Joe and hugged him. Joe introduced Adam to him.

"Adam is a childhood friend from Australia. He'd like to volunteer here for a couple of weeks before returning to Melbourne."

"Hi, Adam. We're all in shock because of the tractor accident. You're lucky you weren't hurt too. Did you see what happened? It's unbelievable. I knew all three of them. What a tragedy. And Dani...?"

"Yes, we saw it all." Joe held back tears, finding it difficult to speak. "It was a miracle the driver survived. I saw him roll away and then get up, bloody but on his feet again."

"It was horrible. Never seen anyone killed or dead bodies before, other than in a coffin at a funeral," Adam added.

"Well, living in this country... I hate to tell you, but you'll see more. You never get used to it, but... but it's part of life here."

Days passed. Shimon returned alone, depressed. A black cloud hung over the kibbutz. Joe thought it was a difficult time to start in a new place, but with Steve's help, he managed to fit in quickly. Joe and Adam were assigned to work in the banana plantation below in El Hama. Joe asked the work coordinator to transfer him to the fishponds nearby, but he refused:

"We need you where you are now," he said.

"But I've studied Marine Biology. I know all about fish," Joe argued.

"That doesn't matter. It's not academic knowledge we need, just strong shoulders to carry bananas. Stay with your Australian friend."

Joe didn't argue.

Going down that snake path every day was scary at first,

after the accident, but they got used to it. Several volunteers had left after the accident; Joe and Adam were needed and valued as workers. Adam extended his stay.

Steve worked as the kibbutz carpenter's assistant. He had a pile of low pine and cane stools he had made himself in the corner of his room. Brightly coloured posters and artwork were displayed on the walls, amongst them a poster of the revolutionary Che Guevara smoking a cigar, prominent above his bed.

The young volunteers would gather in Steve's room after work, tell jokes, drink beer, sometimes play cards or scrabble. Joe played chess with Steve. Adam didn't often join them; he spent most of his time after work in his room, reading. Joe had "kibbutz parents", an older couple with children, but didn't visit them much. Adam accompanied him once, but found it boring. He and Joe began to drift apart after a while.

One day Steve brought out a stick of hashish, grated it, placed the resultant substance in a colourful Indian pipe, lit it and offered it to Joe.

"I don't do drugs."

"Come on Joe, relax. The accident really upset you, didn't it?"

"Yeah, it did. I've never seen anyone killed before."

Steve laughed.

"You're in Israel now. What did you expect? Come on, take a puff!"

"It was just an accident, not a battle or a fedayeen attack!"

"Cool it, man. This will help you unwind. You'll sleep better."

He tried the pipe. His head felt woozy after a few puffs. He didn't like doing something illegal, but he did sleep better that night.

The next time they smoked together Joe told him about Bora and his coat. Steve was fascinated.

"You mean that old coat you wear on cold days is actually a relic from the second world war?"

"Yeah. It even has a bullet hole in it."

"Cool."

Dani never returned to the kibbutz. Rumours went around about what had happened to him. A police investigation discovered that there had been a mechanical fault in the tractor's brakes. Two policemen came up to ask questions in the kibbutz garage. They learned that Dani took care of all repairs to the tractor himself. Joe heard they wanted to charge Dani with criminal negligence, or even manslaughter, but the case was eventually dropped without formal charges.

Dani was rumoured to have had a nervous breakdown and was in a psychiatric hospital. Steve told them that Dani was a war hero, awarded medals for his bravery and was one of the paratroopers who'd stormed the Golan in 1967. In the Yom Kippur War, his unit was decimated; he was one of the few survivors. Joe heard that he had friends high up who hushed up the whole thing and got him off the hook and that the dead volunteers' families weren't interested in pursuing criminal negligence charges; they'd been contacted, had been asked to drop the matter and had agreed. He didn't know what to believe but felt that something was strange in this story.

Three weeks after his dramatic arrival at the kibbutz, Joe was called into the kibbutz office. He walked into the concrete bloc that served both as an office and mail room.

Selma, the secretary, was quite friendly: "Shalom, Yossi. I have something for you here."

"Hi, Selma!"

He looked at the desk between them. It was strewn with papers and letters in disarray, messy like Selma's hair.

"You've got a letter for me?"

"Two. One from your parents, and one that looks kind of official."

She dug around a moment, then pulled something out of the pile and handed Joe an aerogram and a postcard.

"Here they are!"

"Thank you," he said as he stuffed them into his coat pocket and left, excited.

His parents' letter gave their usual greetings, and regards from friends, Judy among them. He felt a pang when he read her name. The card only had a couple of words scrawled on it:

"Welcome to Israel, Yossi. Good luck in your new home."

There was no date or return address. The signature was difficult to read. He deciphered it as "Joseph Borowski."

Bora. He knows where I am! But how do I contact him? This is strange.

Chapter 12
KIBBUTZ DAYS: TIME FOR A DECISION, JENNY

Joe and Adam were working in the banana groves, down in El Hama in the Yarmouk Valley at the corner meeting point of the three borders of Israel, Syria, and Jordan. They went down daily, except Saturdays, at about 5:00 a.m., returning for lunch in the kibbutz around 1 p.m.

Work on the banana plantation was hard. When the bunches were almost ripe, but still hard and green, they were lowered onto the shoulders of the kibbutz workers. A big, sharp knife slashed through the stem that attached the fruit to the tree and then Joe would stagger with his bunch over to a waiting trailer on a dirt road that encircled the trees. There were sometimes accidents, though usually only minor mishaps. Joe knew of no one who had lost a limb, but he had himself almost lost a finger.

He nicked it with just such a knife once while standing on a ladder precariously preparing to cut down a bunch of bananas. The bunch fell to the ground, knocking over his volunteer workmate. The kibbutznik they were working with started yelling at them until he saw the blood dripping from Joe's hand and spreading across the front of his work shirt. After washing and bandaging it in their workers' hut, they flagged down an army jeep which drove him down the snake path to the nearest kibbutz. There he was given a tetanus shot and his hand stitched up.

Most days were uneventful. The daily highlight was the big, jolly breakfast the guys cooked and prepared for themselves in their wooden hut, and the end-of-the-day naked swim in the sulphur baths in El Hama.

Occasional alerts of a possible border crossing by terrorists from Syria or Jordan meant they were not allowed down for that day. On ordinary days, free of any infiltration, a soldier usually armed with an Uzi sub-machine gun, accompanied them to the banana groves.

The kibbutz ran a rifle range. The volunteers could hear the kibbutz members practicing a couple of times a week. Joe would have liked to join them but was told the use of a weapon was only for members, or soldiers stationed there, not foreign volunteers. They were not allowed near the rifle range.

The long hot summer mornings dragged on. The humidity in the valley was high most of the year. The shorter winter days exposed them to blasts of cold wind blowing down the valley as if through a funnel. The banana tree was not great shelter from the elements, so Joe waterproofed the old coat and wore it to work. It provided him with good protection. Giving it to Bora didn't look like it was possible anymore.

Days in the banana plantation had a set monotonous routine in the winter, when there was less to do: spraying insecticides, covering the new fruit with paper bags to protect the nascent bunches from the bugs, and cutting down diseased trees. Michael, the manager, liked Adam and Joe and insisted they stay on, although less workers were needed in the wintertime.

But Joe lost his enthusiasm for the work in the banana groves, and Adam was already planning to return to Australia. The kibbutz had agreed to let Joe have the day off to accompany Adam to the airport. He planned to take advantage of the day out of the kibbutz to visit Rivka and Motti.

Meanwhile, Joe asked to be transferred to the fishponds. He again mentioned his degree in Marine Biology but that seemed to make no impression on the work coordinator or the kibbutz committee.

He did, however, manage to get himself assigned to work with Maurice, the kibbutz gardener. This was a plum job, but most people didn't last long with Maurice. Recently divorced, Maurice was taciturn and unfriendly, sometimes very irritable. He had been wounded in the previous war, walked with a pronounced limp and was also hard of hearing.

Joe didn't mind any of this since it meant he spent a lot of his time working on his own, tending flowerbeds, watering, weeding, and mowing the lawn next to the kibbutz dining hall. He enjoyed the solitude, driving the little lawn tractor back and forth while singing songs to himself. He loved the smell of the freshly cut grass and the glorious view of the Kinneret and Kibbutz Ein Gev down below.

Adam's day of departure arrived and Joe told Maurice that he expected to be back the next day. Adam left on a warm sunny day in late April. Of course, Joe was sad to say goodbye, but understood his friend's desire to return to Melbourne. He missed the city, his family, and sometimes his friends, too.

In the noisy throng at the airport terminal, they managed a brief last conversation:

"Adam, please go visit my mum and dad when you get back, OK?"

"Sure. I was planning to do that!"

"And bring them these photos of the kibbutz, all right? They worry so much. It's really important to show them that everything is OK with me."

Adam nodded, took the photos and stuffed them into his bag. Joe heard the call for boarding Adam's flight over the loudspeaker.

"You've got to go now. You'll write?"

"Of course, I'll write, Joey."

"Are you planning to come back to Israel, Adam?"

"I don't know. That's a hard question to answer. I'm not ready to go to the army just yet."

They hugged and Adam walked away.

Joe left the airport feeling very alone and confused. He decided to keep to his plan to visit Rivka and Motti before heading home. He'd spend that night in Lochamei HaGetaot and return to Afikei Kinneret the next morning. He called them from a public phone.

"Hello, Rivka. It's Yossi. I'd like to come to visit. I've a day off … I'm now at the airport and on my way back to the kibbutz."

"Shalom, Yossi. Nice to hear from you, but it isn't a good time to come."

Rivka's voice was strained.

"Why, what's the matter?"

"Motti is in the hospital. He had a heart attack. I'll be leaving soon to be with him, but he's not allowed to have any other visitors."

"Oh no! What happened?"

"He collapsed at work. Thank God, his workmates got him to the emergency room on time. The doctors say he'll recover but he needs rest now. Soon we'll arrange a visit. I have to go now, my ride to the hospital is here for me."

I can't believe it. Motti is a robust guy. He looks so strong and healthy. Poor Rivka. How will she manage? She's so sensitive and so dependent on him.

Joe travelled back to Afikei Kinneret, worried, obsessing about Motti.

Motti was released from the hospital a week later with strict instructions for lifestyle changes. Rivka made sure that happened; she kept visitors away for a while to let him, and herself, rest and recuperate for a few more weeks.

"I got a call from Yossi while you were in the hospital. He wanted to visit us. He said he was on his way back to the kibbutz from the airport. His friend, Adam, was returning to Melbourne," Rivka said.

"You should have let him come, Rivka. I'd love to see the kid and hear how he's doing on that new kibbutz of his."

"But you need to rest, Motti. Doctor's orders."

"Call him and tell to come as soon as he gets another day off, please," he insisted.

When Joe did visit a month later, he walked the familiar path from the bus stop near the dining hall to Rivka and Motti's cottage, enjoying the scent of roses until he saw Rivka tending to their herb garden.

"How are you, Yossi? We're so glad that you were able to find time to see us. Motti has been looking forward to this day with you."

"I'm fine now, but I was sad to see my friend, Adam, leave Israel."

"They say new friends are like silver, but old friends are like gold."

"I like that saying. Where's it from?"

"It's Talmudic. And... are you happy on your new kibbutz?"

"Yes. Now I'm working as a gardener. It's more interesting than bananas."

"A young lady in your life?"

"Yes."

Rivka smiled, knowingly.

"I haven't had a chance to tell you, but I've heard from Bora."

Rivka's smile broadened.

"Really. How so?" She sounded quizzical.

"He sent me a postcard welcoming me to my new kibbutz but no address or other contact information."

"I'm not surprised. That's his style. You looked annoyed telling me that."

"I am. I don't like his mysterious behaviour."

"Well, Yossi, patience is a virtue. With Bora, that's your only option."

"Enough about mystery, Rivka, tell me about Motti."

"Come, let's go inside. Just knowing that you were going to visit with us has really cheered him up."

Yossi was shocked to see how much weight Motti had lost, how frail he'd become. He saw the walker beside the entrance as he came into their place. He also observed that Rivka was well organized around his care. She, already tall, seemed to have grown taller still. He noticed the line of medication bottles on the shelf by Motti's bed and that Rivka didn't bring out cake this time, just fruit.

Motti read his concerned look:

"I'm fine, Yossi. Don't worry so much! I have an angel here watching my health."

Rivka laughed.

"You have to take care of your health yourself, old man!"

Motti gave her a long, loving look and then turned back to Yossi.

"How goes it on that new kibbutz of yours?"

"For now, I'm a gardener. I like it. I wanted to work at the fishpond, but that wasn't possible."

"Sounds good. Are you still hoping to find Bora?" Motti asked.

"Ah… Yes, I am…" Yossi replied, but he didn't feel as confident as he'd been when he first arrived, and heard his own hesitation. "I told Rivka that I got a postcard from him, very mysterious though."

"And how about girls?" Motti asked, apparently wanting to change the subject.

"I've met someone I like. Her name's Jenny."

"Aha! That is good news."

■■■

Jenny was a Canadian volunteer, a friend of Steve's, who ran the members' club house, which they call the "moadon." She was pretty and kind, her smile infectious. Steve introduced Joe to her before he left for Toronto.

It was a hot Friday afternoon. The usual crowd was sitting around drinking beer at Steve's when she came into the room. She was petite, wearing a short crimson skirt, and a black halter top, a light purple scarf draped across her otherwise bare shoulders, her auburn hair cut to a length just above them. Joe couldn't take his eyes off her.

"Hi, guys! A beer party again?"

They grunted, "hello."

Joe was embarrassed by the rudeness of these guys to this pretty girl. He took an immediate liking to her when he heard her relaxed response:

"Well, enjoy your beer. We have a guest performance of a jazz group in the moadon this evening at eight. Please come. It's going to be fun. They're good. I just heard them practicing. And there's more beer and snacks for you too!"

Her sparkling eyes and warm, infectious smile lit Joe's imagination.

Wow! I'd like to get to know her more. She's got real presence, and self-confidence.

"Wait, Jenny, there's someone new here I want you to meet. Jenny, this is Joe from Melbourne, Australia." Joe managed a friendly smile. "He's been here a few days and is just settling in. Joe, this is Jenny, a fellow Canadian who runs our kibbutz club house."

"Hi Joe! Welcome. Come around to the moadon sometime and we'll get to know each other better."

"That's an invitation I'll follow up on for sure!"

"Got to get back to work. Look forward to seeing all of you there, later. See ya's!"

After that, Joe started coming to the moadon regularly after work, just to see her.

Steve's departure saddened Joe as they had become good friends, but Steve's mother had developed cancer. He had to fly home.

"You'll come back, Steve, won't you?"

"I don't know, Joe. I loved living on the kibbutz, and I like the communal lifestyle, but the militarism here disturbs me. I've got to think about it all."

"What do you mean by "militarism"? Israel is not militaristic!"

Steve laughed.

"If you stay long enough, you'll see. My family needs me now. Did I tell you that they're Holocaust survivors too, like your parents? They're freaking out because I'm here."

"No, I don't remember ever talking about that."

Joe's face showed his surprise.

"Oh, I guess we didn't talk about it. You know that if you accept Israeli citizenship, they'll conscript you."

"I know. That freaks out my parents too."

"You want to go to the army?"

"Not sure, maybe."

Steve left on a dark, rainy morning. Joe, wrapped in his Bora coat, waited with him under the bus shelter until an empty bus, its lights blinding, skidded into the kibbutz parking lot, splashing them both. Shivering as they shook off the spray, they walked towards the vehicle.

"You'll write Steve, yeah?"

"Of course. And you write and tell me how things go with Jenny."

"Sure. Take care of yourself, Joe."

They shook hands. Steve picked up his things and went up the bus's steps.

Joe, buried in the old fur coat, waved, and watched Steve wave goodbye through the window. The bus drove away into the mist.

Will I ever see him again? First Nancy left, then Adam, now Steve...who's next? Will Jenny be gone soon too?

Weeks later at supper, Joe overheard some of the "Anglos", that's what they called the English speakers, talking excitedly about their impending army service. Pretty Jenny was sitting there surrounded by a bunch of guys, holding her own in the conversation. Joe was still struggling to get her attention, she had so many other admirers.

He brought his tray over to join them and sat down next to Dov, from London, his friend from his banana plantation days. Dov made aliya a year earlier through a Zionist youth group and had immediately accepted Israeli citizenship. His "call-up" notice had arrived recently, which is what led to the gathering that evening.

"I'm going to Nahal," Dov said.

"Me too!" Mike, the Scotsman piped in.

"What's Nahal?" Joe asked, raising his voice to be heard over the din of the dining room.

"That's the acronym for Fighting Pioneer Youth in Hebrew... combines combatant military service with time on a new settlement," Jenny explained.

"We know all that!" chorused Harry and Sandy, the Americans – he always confused their names.

Roger, the Kiwi, explained: "As soldiers without families, they call us Hayalim Bodedim, we get to do part of our service on our own kibbutz. Right here."

"Sounds like a good deal," Joe commented.

Seeing Jenny eating heartily reminded Joe to eat. He hadn't

touched his food yet. He took a bite of his cold omelette, then exclaimed: "Great. You'll be here as part of your army service!?"

"Yep. Why don't you two join us. That way you'll get to be with friends during training and active service," Dov suggested, looking first at Joe, then at Jenny.

"Don't know if I'm ready," Joe responded.

"Maybe I will. I'm already an Israeli citizen. I bet they'd take me if I volunteered." Jenny sounded serious.

Joe was impressed by her self-confidence, but army service was a serious issue. He was sorry that Steve wasn't with them anymore to lighten things up. He remembered his cynical comments about the army, and his knack for telling jokes.

Afterwards, on the way out of the dining hall, Joe and Dov got to talking.

"Hey, Joe, you sounded interested yourself. Do you want to come join us? We're going down to the army conscription office next Monday."

"No. I wasn't planning to be in the army yet since I've only been here a couple of months, and haven't taken on Israeli citizenship. I'm still an Australian citizen. Isn't it a problem to go to the army here?"

"There's an arrangement set up. You'd be conscripted, not volunteer, and wouldn't lose your Australian citizenship. Think about it. Wouldn't it be more fun to go with a bunch of guys you know?"

"Fun! The army, fun? What are you talking about!? Armies have lots of discipline, and they're about killing people, aren't they?"

"The Israeli army is different. It's less formal, and it's about self-defence. After what happened to the Jews in Europe, it's clear that we need an army of our own. They lost a lot of soldiers in the Yom Kippur war. We're needed."

"But they need me here on the kibbutz. When you guys go, they'll need my work even more than before..."

"Just think about it. It'd be great if you joined us..."

Dov and Joe parted, each to his own room in the row of grey

prefabricated boxes that served the foreign volunteers.

Dov had decorated his space with coloured bottles and a grape vine he'd nurtured growing over the entrance that created shade for his old cane rocking chair.

Joe's room was much sparer, bare of anything superfluous, but he did have plans for future improvements. He wanted to invest some time on his own garden, plant something, but got home from work tired every day and fell asleep until supper. He remembered, was inspired by Rivka's garden.

Joe had trouble relaxing after that conversation. He was preoccupied, obsessed with thoughts of army service. The stories of his parents' and their friends' resistance against the Germans in the war kept reverberating through his mind. Suddenly, he thought of Bora again, and his imagined dashing, heroic acts of defiance and revenge... Dov's words made sense, but, on the other hand, he'd always hated militarism and nationalistic jingoism, had protested Australian involvement in Vietnam. He felt tense, tried reading, but couldn't focus, kept reading the same paragraph over and over again.

He put on his kibbutz slippers, and a light jacket, and went outside.

He wandered around for a while, looking at the lights twinkling in the distance down below. He headed for the moadon. Jenny would be sitting there. She was always good to talk to.

"I'm going to the army with the guys," she told him, her face alight with determination.

He wasn't surprised, but wondered whether this wasn't a reason for him to join too.

"I can't discuss it right now, Joe," she said responding to the look on his face.

"I'm too pressured for time. I have to put things away and then need to go out right away."

"Go out where?" he asked.

"To meet with someone, to go for a walk with her. There are some issues to resolve. Come on, smile! We will talk later, I promise. OK?"

"All right," he said despondently.

He sat there alone trying to watch television. But the panel discussion about Moshe Dayan's failings as Minister of Defence didn't interest him. He turned the thing off, went back to his room. The only light still glowing in that dark row of singles' dormitories was his own. A dog barked from the other side of the kibbutz, echoed by answering barks of other canines from different directions around the settlement.

He kicked off his slippers and got into bed, still in his clothes. He tossed and turned for a long time. When he finally fell asleep it must have been three in the morning. He dreamed that a strange man, wearing his partisan coat, spoke to him, that he told him to "be a man", to go to the army. "But the army is no place of freedom!" he argued with him in his dream.

It was not long until someone knocked on the door. It was Dov, calling him to come out to work.

"Joe, Get up, man! Get up, you lazy bum. It's five-thirty. They're waiting for us out there!"

Joe had trouble opening his eyes, putting on his boots in a blur, but remembered what he'd been thinking about when he fell asleep. He now knew what he'd do. He was going to the army too, with Dov, and the guys, and Jenny. He would prove himself, live up to Bora's example, be free, be a man.

The next day Jenny went down to the army offices and registered, hoping to go in with the guys. They added her to the "lonely soldiers" group from Afikei Kinneret.

Joe followed her example the day after that.

Chapter 13

JOURNEY TO ARMY SERVICE

Early Monday morning, Joe got into the van with the other guys. Heavy Harry sat down first, dropping down the folding bench. Dov folded down the other one and sat just behind the driver. Joe could see Shimon's head through the half-open internal sliding window next to his friend's shoulder. The rest sat facing each other on either side of Harry and Dov. They were all shorn and shaved, looked different. Dov's face, without his thick black beard, looked ghostly white. "Like a plucked chicken," Joe thought to himself.

Each of them brought a bag of things they'd been advised to bring by army veterans on the kibbutz: toiletries, changes of underwear and socks, pocketknives, small screwdrivers, bits of string, sewing kits, and reading matter.

Joe had packed "One Day in the Life of Ivan Denisovich" by Alexander Solzhenitsyn. It was the story of a prisoner in the Soviet gulag struggling to survive in a repressive environment. Having decided to join the group going to the army, he had changed his status in the country to citizen and signed papers requesting an early conscription. He had received his call-up notice on the spot in Tiberias a week earlier, the day after Jenny's notice arrived.

There was no turning back now. He could feel his nervousness, that he was scared. He looked around him. The other guys were serious and silent too; no one was smiling. Each of them sat there looking contemplative, not looking at the others. He'd been told that the first weeks in basic training were rough, that they broke you down as an individual to build you up as a soldier. Now they were going to find out what that meant. He wanted to get there sooner to get started with it all, but Shimon was driving more carefully than usual down this familiar but dangerous route.

The journey seemed to take forever. He looked past Shimon's silhouetted head through the front window. It was the only way to see outside this otherwise windowless van. He saw the rocky basalt Golan slopes and the dry, thorn-filled fields slowly passing by. He saw some rusted barbed wire fencing and signs warning of old Syrian mines.

They went around a couple of familiar hairpin curves. They were approaching the area of the accident. He looked out the window again and was shocked to see the burnt-out remains of the tractor, melted, its torn, black wheels upturned, moving in the wind like the legs of a dead cockroach. And were those remnants of the smashed trailer? Three lives were lost here. And how many have been lost in the Israeli army? How many young people had died in uniform, or were wearing no uniform at all when they perished? He closed his eyes, sighed, and tried to think of something else.

Dov elbowed him and whispered, "What's the matter, Joey? You're not feeling well?"

Joe hated being called that. It sounded so like his childhood friends. He wanted to be someone else now, not the Caulfield boy he'd been. Not Yossi, not Joey, just plain old Joe.

"Call me Joe or Yosef, not Joey, please! Ah, I'm fine... eh... remembering Dani's accident. We just passed the place where it happened. I just saw it, the tractor, it's still out there."

"Yeah. It was horrible. I remember that day. The kibbutz has fewer volunteers since then and is obsessed with safety on this road. The kibbutz executive committee won't let just anyone drive down here now, only experienced drivers like Shimon. It's good they're careful, but they should've been before, no?"

Joe nodded but remained silent. His mind carried him back to the scene on the day of the accident. He clenched the seat beside him while breathing deeply and trying to release the tension...

They continued in silence, Shimon still driving cautiously down the steep road. He turned on the radio. They heard the recitation of the morning Shema prayer, the familiar peeps, the morning theme tune, then listened to the news: no special news, just another car collision down south... a family on their way back from a wedding... father and mother killed; three children orphaned. Sad.

Shimon said nothing.

Joe thought about that family's tragedy. Remembered that his family had experienced a few tragedies in the past too. Before he was born.

Shimon turned the car radio off. It was 6:00 a.m.

They reached Tiberias, drove down Jerusalem Boulevard and turned into Hofein Street. Shimon pulled up opposite the army offices, waiting at the wheel, engine still running, as they got out of the van.

Passers-by stared at the little crowd of young men and women gathering outside the army conscription office. It grew larger as more cars pulled up to drop people off. A delivery truck blocked the road for a while causing a lot of shouting and honking until the swarthy tattooed truck driver got the message and moved out of the way. He dropped a lit cigarette out the window as he drove away.

Joe remembered the emotional scenes when Jewish parents left their kids behind for summer camp in Melbourne. His parents and their friends related to every parting as ominous, were overprotective, and he knew why, but this was real. Soldiers kill and get killed, there are accidents, this isn't summer camp.

He saw tearful women parting from sons and daughters, crying younger brothers and sisters watching helplessly as grown men, pride and fear in their eyes, hugged their offspring before letting them go. Parents and older siblings were giving last words of advice, handing small parcels of food to the new conscripts. Many of the new recruits looked impatient with the family fuss, wanting them to leave, others were reluctant to let them go.

He watched a young woman tie a pendant on red string around the neck of her son. The son, who looked too slight to be a soldier, had maybe never shaved, was fingering the gift when Joe heard the woman say, "It's for good luck, Shmuel." She kissed him, bawling and shuddering, as he tried to pull away from her. He was obviously embarrassed, wanted her to go.

Only their little group of "lone soldiers" was unaccompanied.

No one came to see them off. They just had each other.

Shimon got back behind the wheel of the van, reignited the engine that he had meanwhile turned off. He got out, disgruntled, loudly slammed the van door shut after they collected their bags, then waved, calling out:

"Good luck, hevreh!"

And drove off.

Joe had never experienced a lonelier moment in his life. He barely knew the guys with him. His parents and sister, his childhood friends were so far away from him on this day. They knew nothing of this scene he was witnessing of families sacrificing their sons and daughters to the Israeli military. He could only imagine how they would react but preferred not to think about it.

"What have I done?" he asked himself, looking at the Egged buses whose presence he now noticed, their engines purring, waiting to swallow them. He realized that they had been prepared nearby all that time. Two soldiers came to collect them, to shoo away the families, after some perfunctory words of greeting and encouragement, and the checking of lists and identification. It was already 7:30 a.m.

"Welcome to the I.D.F.! You're now army property. Get On!" a soldier with a couple of stripes on his arm yelled.

His mate sneered at them: "We're leaving for Bakum in ten minutes. Hurry, throw your shit in, Move it!"

A mass of young men, women and bags pushing and shoving disappeared into the bus in minutes. Their families started to leave. Joe thought he saw a man hovering behind the little crowd who looked familiar, reminded him of the photo of Bora he'd been shown, but he wasn't sure. The man was gone when he looked outside again.

In the bus, they were arranged by groups, all the kibbutz guys in one section. He sat down next to Dov, with whom he exchanged a few words. They were both soon snoring, Dov leaning on the window, he, on Dov's shoulder.

He was awoken by a loudspeaker blaring military marching music. The bus drove through a large metal gate surrounded by barbed wire around which were shops and stalls selling drinks, fast food, and small souvenirs to a crowd of soldiers and their families. A sign read "Bakum – Tel Hashomer, I.D.F. base for sorting and induction". They had reached their destination.

They drove into the base, along a well-surfaced road, passed many gates and compounds, and another area of shops, until they arrived at an immense parking area. They'd entered an alternative world, a city for soldiers and officers, multitudes walking or marching past them in every direction.

"Everybody off the bus!" a handlebar-moustached sergeant shouted at them after the bus door flew open. He saw the three stripes with a red star on top of them on the man's sleeve. The sergeant's boots were so shiny he could see a soldier's reflection in them.

Joe was pushed out the door by a human wave of young bodies and limbs. He struggled to stay on his feet and to see over the heads around him, to see where he was and where they were headed.

Dov called over to him from over another's head, laughing: "We're in the army now!"

"Yeah, what fun!" Joe yelled back.

Dov shoved through the crowd to join him, arriving out of breath.

"This place is huge! Did you see all the soldiers walking around? So many bases... I even saw a cinema, and lots of chicks here too."

"You two, shut up!" the sergeant barked at them.

Joe and Dov were marched into a long wooden building. The new recruits were being processed inside along a long table. The soldiers, mostly girls, did not smile much and looked bored. Joe was asked to present his call-up papers and identity card to the first freckled one, sitting, waiting impatiently for him to come up to her.

"Australia?"

"Yes..."

She laughed.

"Don't stand there scratching your balls!" she yelled, having checked him off against a list of names. "Move on!"

They were so young, and no one explained anything. It felt like a conveyor belt for creating soldiers out of civilians. The next one, a stooped guy with acne, shoved a paper at him to sign, then pointed to another table. There a smiling girl soldier made Joe roll up his sleeves and without further warning he was given an injection in each arm, and yet another soldier gave him a new paper to sign. At a third, a long trestle table, there were piles of things that each of the recruits had to collect according to size and unit: a kitbag, boots, two khaki trousers and two olive-green shirts, socks, a sweater, a jacket, (all marked I.D.F., but made in the USA), a cloth belt, plastic cup and metal cutlery.

"Take your mesting!" shouted a short bespectacled girl, shoving a metal box with a handle at him."

"The... what?"

"Move on!" she growled.

Weeks passed until he figured out that "mesting" was Hebrew for the "mess-tin" out of which he had been eating his rushed meals during training.

Having also signed a paper for these things he and the others were directed to a side room behind a long khaki-coloured curtain where they had to strip, put on a uniform, and stow the rest in the kitbag. Jenny had meanwhile disappeared. He'd seen her auburn hair going into a section for girls from which he heard giggling.

He'd lost Dov, too, in the confusion, but saw that Harry was nearby. Harry looked comical in clothes too tight for his big frame. He went back to argue but returned still wearing his ill-fitting outfit. Joe was luckier; his clothes were the right size. There were advantages to being of medium height and of medium build.

Joe emerged, dragging his kitbag, at the far end of this factory-like wooden processing hall. The new recruits were directed by the same moustachioed sergeant with the bright, polished boots to waiting bus-like army vehicles. Another waiting soldier with two stripes on his arm checked them off lists and sent them to a bus labelled "Nahal."

Joe looked at this corporal as he walked past him. He looked very familiar. Then he realized. It was Charlie!

"Charlie, what are you doing here?!"

"What do you think I am doing, Joe! You can see, can't you?" Charlie laughed.

They hugged.

"Are you headed to the Nahal base?" Charlie asked.

"Yeah, that's right. I can't believe it's you. How did you end up here, of all places!?"

"Oh. I'm here temporarily, but I'll be returning to the Nahal base in a couple of days. I'll look for you there. Can't talk now. Go, get on the bus already."

"Yes, sir! See ya' soon."

Joe saluted his friend in an exaggerated fashion, laughing.

"See you, soldier!"

Joe got on the bus, found Dov inside waiting for him, and told him he'd met a friend out there, who might, if they're lucky, help them when they get to their army base.

"Sounds good, Joe."

Dov wasn't smiling any more.

Joe looked around him at the rows of uniformed men and women, had trouble recognizing the guys he'd come with. He saw Jenny looking boyish, her hair tied up in a bun; she didn't look happy either, sitting in a back corner of the bus with a bunch of other girls from neighbouring settlements. They were wearing khaki-green, all sitting silently, waiting. He waved. She waved back, forcing a smile.

"We're soldiers now," Harry said.

"Duh. That's kind of obvious," Joe responded.

"Cannon fodder," commented a guy behind them, frowning.

"Hello. Do we know you?" Joe asked the new soldier, noticing his piercing dark eyes and sharp facial features.

"I'm Nicky, from Kibbutz Maagan. Got here through Hashomer Hatzair, but my settlement group fell apart. I'm the only one left. The rest went back to England."

"Yeah. I heard about that. Nice to meet you, Nicky. I'm Joe. This here is Dov."

"Hi! I know who you are. From Afikei Kinneret, right? I knew your friend Steve. He told me to look out for you. We met once before at a concert at Ein Gev a couple of months ago. You came with Steve."

"Ah… Yes. I remember now. You're a writer, or an artist or something."

"I write poetry. I've had a few things published in the past."

Joe was impressed. Dov less so. In any case, they all shook hands.

A little later Joe slid his book out of his jacket pocket and started reading, wondering how a poet would survive the army experience.

Chapter 14

ARMY LIFE

The "One Day in the Life..." book was getting tattered. Joe carried it around in his jacket pocket. He felt a sense of disjoint, even absurdity of what he was reading. Solzhenitsyn's book, describing the sufferings of the simple peasant Sukhov in a Soviet concentration camp in Siberia, was a source of escape and calm in an army. Weird, but true. Whenever he had the chance, he'd read at least a few lines.

Joe remembered walking around Monash University campus with biology books in his spacious Bora coat pockets. Now he was carrying Ivan Denisovitch around in an army jacket.

The annoying yelling of orders, the endless standing in line waiting, the stupid physical "punishments" their N.C.O.s gave them ("ten sit-ups! Now!"; "Twenty press-ups, right away!"; "You have five minutes on the clock to run around that building and back. Go!"), the many little humiliations ("Lazy bum!"; "fatso, move your arse!"), the mindless constant physical chores ("Hey, you, soldier, move that rock here!"; "paint that tree trunk white"; "repaint it, it's not good enough!"), the limited time to sleep or eat, the boring guard duty at night, the institutional food, all these were hard, but they were nothing compared to what he was reading about, or compared to the stories he grew up hearing from his parents and their friends!

As a student, Joe had read Elie Wiesel's "Night", a horrific description of "life" in Auschwitz, in the shadow of the chimneys. This book he was reading reminded him of that dehumanization and brutality, not of where he was now, suffering the prosaic reality of an induction and submergence into army life. Ivan reminded him of why the Jews needed an army of their own, and why he was in it.

But these thoughts evaporated with time, as the lack of sleep and nagging hunger during basic training got the better of him. Sometimes, despite himself, he did see similarities, realized that he, too, was being – if only temporarily – dehumanized.

He began to resent, even hate, the army.

Going home for the "weekend" – only a day and a half – Friday afternoon and Shabbat or being rewarded with the gift of a short "after" (one evening or half-day off) became his strongest desire as the cycles of training ground him down each long, sweaty, exhausting week.

On those "weekends" when they didn't go home, watching the other soldiers go home was upsetting. He was filled with envy watching their joyful faces as they were granted leave, received their "passes." He saw how quickly they ran out of the gates of the base to go home, while he and his friends stayed behind in their army base.

The weekly "misdar", the end-of-the-week ritual in which all platoons were assembled to stand in formation waiting for the anticipated announcement from the Lieutenant (the "mem-peh") as to who would get leave, and who would not, was one of the experiences he hated most. He resented the use of denial of leave as a stick with which to beat them. Worse was returning to the dusty, grey tents after that event. The eventual return to the army base after leave was still worse than that. That moment when one's heart sunk seeing the gate of the base again… after getting off the bus. It was depressing.

There were regular visitors' days once every few weeks. Parents and families came to see their sons or daughters. On days like those, Joe felt acutely the loneliness of the "lonely soldier" and wished he was not there. Shared gifts of drinks, cookies, cakes, or fruit from those whose families came were kind and much appreciated but did not reduce the sense of abandonment. They made it worse. He once called Rivka and Motti in desperation but hung up before they answered. He was sure they would come if he asked them to, but he didn't feel right doing so.

Three weeks before the end of basic training, on the last visitor's day the familiar battered old Peugeot van finally drove into the base assembly area. Shimon got out and opened the sliding door, from which Selma, Maurice and a couple of volunteers emerged. Selma, with her usual good cheer, took charge of setting out a folding table and some chairs and putting out a spread for "our soldiers." Joe, Dov, Jenny, and the others were delighted to see them and dug into the goodies they brought with gusto, saving some things to share with other less fortunate rookies later in the tents.

Motti and Rivka never came, which Joe understood. They sent greeting cards and visited him on the kibbutz twice while he was there but never set foot in the army base itself. Once, while on leave at Afikei Kinneret, Selma brought him a small parcel, unmarked with no return address. He opened it to find a small chess set inside and an attached note which read "Good luck in the army!" It was initialled with the letter B, otherwise unsigned, but he recognized the writing. Bora. He learned to cherish it over the next couple of years.

The army organized extra food for Shabbat meals, someone made the Kiddush blessing with wine. The day felt special, and the religious guys did some singing too. Weekend newspapers were delivered for the soldiers to share every Friday, and in the second month, the volunteer soldiers' support group, called Vaad Lemaan Hahayal, delivered playing cards, backgammon, and board games, but none of these special times, nor the treats and gifts, could counter the awful feeling of having been denied his freedom.

On other days, when he had spare time, he would wander away from their tents looking for a quiet escape to read in solitude but wherever he went, there were fences, barbed wire, notices saying most places were out-of-bounds to the new recruits.

He once saw a white butterfly, with orange markings on its wings, on the other side of the fence flitting through the yellow flowers growing there. He would have liked to have been on the other side, too, free to fly away like that beautiful creature.

He felt imprisoned in this ugly army base with its rows of tents set in concrete floors, stinking toilets, and ever-present military discipline. Some of the locally born soldiers had "protektzia." With these "connections", they were able to enjoy an extra "after" – the short leave – or a family visit at odd times. The "hayalim bodedim" from overseas missed out on the benefits that came with protektzia.

Another day, and another, passed.

The sun rose, and the sun set. The lunar months went through their cycle, as they always had, from a thin sliver to a quarter, then a half-moon, then a shining full moon and back through its declining stages until there was but a sliver again, facing the other way in the night sky, and then it was gone. He learned about the renewing "new moon" and its significance from one of the religious soldiers on guard duty one night.

Through the four months of basic training, Joe and his friends were exposed to the elements, were taught the rudiments of military lore and skills, were disciplined and toughened and taught to shoot an M16 rifle, an Uzi, heavier machine guns (05, 03), a mortar and a handheld Lowe missile, to throw hand grenades, to crawl under fences, to run through sand and mud, to crawl through thorns on scraped and bloodied elbows and knees, to take cover behind rocks, to climb walls, to defend and attack positions, and to follow orders.

Joe lost weight, added muscle, and grew his own military moustache. He learned not to volunteer, to be cynical, and to let go of his soft liberal ideals. In imitation of the Israel-born sabras in their unit, even "Zionism" became a dirty word never to be used without an accompanying cutting joke. It translated as "blah blah" for them.

"So where are you from, soldier?" they would ask him sometimes.

His answer, "I am from Melbourne, Australia," brought reactions of disbelief, even scorn.

"You're mad! Why did you come here? I dream of immigrating to New Zealand, or Australia, when I get out of the army" was a refrain he often heard from the Israeli-born soldiers.

The toilet walls were decorated with graffiti counting the days until end of service and cursing the army officers. Every time they were painted over with whitewash, new ones appeared again with accompanying vulgar illustrations. He learned the expressions "Ya Manaayak!" and "Ya Manyak! from reading these anonymous inscriptions; such words were probably remnants of British presence in the Holy Land he was once told.

One day a card arrived in the mail from Rivka. Her handwriting was beautiful. She wrote:

Dear Yossi,

I hope you are well. Army service for everyone is challenging but for you who did not grow up here I'm sure it has its special challenges. Anytime you want to call and talk we would be happy to hear from you. You have warm regards from Motti, and from your mother. She's worried about you. Your father sends his love.

And you have regards from Bora. He called to ask about you, how you were doing in the army and whether you had received the chess set.

Take care of yourself, Yossi!

Rivka xxxx

Bora again. Now in the army there was nothing he could do about finding him.

Joe developed a reputation as a good, disciplined soldier, excelling in the physical fitness demanded of him, competing to surge ahead in the nightly runs, learning to enjoy his growing strength and skills in handling weapons, shooting well. He kept his feelings to himself, determined to fit in, but harbouring doubts he shared with no one.

Dov and Harry weren't like that. They argued and were repeatedly punished for daring to do so. Harry was slow-moving and often late. Dov always had something to say when it was inappropriate, which was most of the time. It was he who started with the responses of "Ken Ha-my-fuck-head" instead of the expected "Ken Hamefaked", which means "Yes, sir" to the amusement of those who, unlike Sergeant Eli, knew English. It took a while until he understood why the guys were snickering. When he did, Dov suffered.

They heard that Jenny in the girls' camp was also getting into trouble, that she spent a couple of days in the base lock-up for unloading her anger and answering back her officers. Joe worried about her as he knew what a sharp tongue she sometimes had. But the girls' quarters were out-of-bounds, and when they did go home that week, she was kept back as a punishment.

Despite his childhood punctuality problems – he'd often been punished for late-coming in school – he came on time. Though he was naturally slow in the morning, he learned to be quick, to be dressed and out of the tent in minutes. (They were officially given seven minutes to do that).

He did pick up some survival skills. Reading at every opportunity helped him stay sane. He always carried a notebook and a pencil. When he could, he'd sketch his fellow soldiers, or objects that caught his attention. He sketched Dov, Harry and Nicky, the poet, their sergeant Eli, their physical fitness trainer Shula, who was called the Madasit, as well as interesting rocks, trees, and a lizard he spied stretched in the sun, baking.

After he "got his eye in", and learned how things worked, he saw that there were opportunities to snatch some real time for himself. Whenever sent on an errand, or given a duty (kitchen, toilets, general cleaning, helping unload truck deliveries) or just during official "rest" times, such as Shabbats and holidays on the base, he would take his book in one of his jacket or pants pockets. If he found a quiet, concealed spot, he would slip his book out and read for a few minutes, or doze.

After the shocking news of a suicide by one of the rookies in another unit during the sixth week of training, the officers started letting up a bit. They heard a rumour that a junior officer who had been sadistically picking on that guy was court-martialled, demoted, and jailed.

Joe finished reading the Solzhenitsyn book and awaited leave to replace it with something less depressing. He needed a new pencil and notebook, having filled his notebook with sketches. They wouldn't let the rookies near the store, "Shekem", to buy anything.

He remembered meeting Charlie at the Tel Hashomer base, on the day he was conscripted, remembered that he might be on the same base somewhere.

He kept an eye out for him, which wasn't easy as the eagle-eyed non-commissioned officers were always ready to pounce on and "discipline" rookies. He avoided standing in public places, looked for safe hiding places from which to peep in search of Charlie but weeks went by with no sight of him.

And then one day he spotted him standing outside the Shekem in a line of soldiers waiting below the window, hoping to buy themselves cigarettes or sweets. He saw someone who looked like Charlie, but this soldier had a crocheted kippa on his head. Could that be him?

The window opened with a loud bang, as the shutter rolled up, and the pushing and shoving started. He could see the familiar freckled face and sandy hair more clearly now as the soldier climbed the wooden step up to the window, watched him leaning on the ledge until the harried soldier inside served him a pack of cigarettes and matches. Yes, it was him.

From his hiding place between two buildings Joe called out to Charlie as he strolled by, smoking. His friend stopped and turned but couldn't see Joe until he emerged from the shadows.

"What're you doing here? It's out-of-bounds here for you rookies."

Charlie took his arm and pulled him back between the buildings.

"How's it going, Joe?"

Charlie offered him a cigarette.

"No thanks. I don't smoke."

Charlie blew out a smoke ring.

"What's that on your head, Charlie?"

"It's a long story, but, in short, I became observant, and started keeping Shabbat…"

"When? What's the story?"

"Not now, Joe. I've got to get back."

Charlie dug into his jacket pocket and produced a bar of chocolate and offered Joe a piece.

"Listen, I really must go, but… are you on the base this Shabbat?

111

"Yes, I am."

"I'm duty officer this weekend. We can talk after dinner on Friday night."

Although Joe was unhappy about again being stuck on the base for Shabbat, that his old friend would be the duty officer this time was good news. He was intrigued that Charlie had become religious, wanted to understand why.

Shabbat came with its usual boredom but this time with the hope of seeing Charlie again.

After the guys released for the "weekend" had left, Joe returned to his empty tent, and sank into the despondency of Friday afternoon in the army, waiting to be assigned his guard duty. He set up his chess set to play but no one from the other tents wanted to. Towards evening he put the chess pieces away and with the remaining soldiers set out for dinner in the army mess. The room they entered, lit by blinding neon lights, was, despite the standard flowers and white tablecloths, ugly.

At the head table sat the officers left behind on duty for the weekend, Charlie, now sporting a moustache, and a large khaki yarmulke amongst them. He was asked to recite the Kiddush prayer over the wine. Some soldiers stood up enthusiastically, others got up slowly, appeared to be bored, a couple of guys remained sitting, defiant.

Joe stood.

When Charlie recited the words from the Torah, reminding of the creation story: "And on the seventh day God rested..." Joe felt something, a stirring, inside. He observed Charlie's face, saw how lit up it was, saw the serene joy in his eyes. He would have liked to question Charlie then and there, but the officers and the "rookies" were at different tables. He'd have to wait with his questions.

After the meal some of the soldiers, including Charlie, led the others in singing, and then recited the grace after meals. Joe found this entertaining, but it felt strange and alien. He told himself that this was all very nice, but it was a kind of escapism, didn't change the reality of the army life they would have to go back to in the coming week, didn't answer his existential issues of death and suffering in an unjust world. And the food wasn't good so why should he sing and express gratitude?

They dispersed. As they left the building, someone poked him from behind. He turned around ready to lash out angrily, but it was Charlie! Despite the religious look, there were the same familiar freckles, blonde hair, and mischievous smile that he knew.

"Shabbat Shalom, Joe. Did that cheer you up a bit?"

"Gut Shabbes, Charlie, but I don't get it. What's happened to you?"

"It's like this, Joe. I was invited to spend time with my mother's cousins in Bnei Brak when I first arrived in Israel."

"Bnei Brak? But that's where all those dosim live – the ultra-orthodox extremists. And they don't go to the army, either!"

"Yeah. I don't agree with them on that, but…"

"I couldn't imagine spending any time with them. How could you do it? They're like the black hats of Ripponlea back in Melbourne, living in their own little ghetto, cut off from the world…"

"I had nowhere else to stay and they were very nice to me. I started going to a shule with them, and to Torah classes. Observing Shabbat added something to my life that I didn't have before. I love singing at the Shabbat meals."

"You're kidding me. That pious stuff?"

"Look, Joe, it's hard to explain. There's something in it. How about we do a Shabbat together when we're on leave. I could invite you to friends and you can see how you like it."

Joe could restrain himself no longer, he raised his voice:

"Now you sound like a missionary – like one of those Lubavitchers. No thanks, Charlie. Not for me!"

He was now yelling and waving his hands. A couple of passing soldiers turned to stare at them.

Charlie laughed nervously.

"Cool it, Joe. No one is missionizing you. Suit yourself, but if you change your mind…"

"Thanks anyway. I've got to get back to my tent…"

Chapter 15

ARMY INCIDENTS

For their advanced infantry training they were moved from the greenery of their basic training base down to a dusty, desolate base in the southern Negev. There were no butterflies there, just sand. Discipline had eased up, but it was physically gruelling. They got home less often. When he could, Joe wrote to Jenny who now was elsewhere in medics training. Her few letters signed "love, Jenny" put a smile on his face despite the hardship. He hoped that was true for her too.

Training was interrupted once for a few days to send their platoon to participate in riot control in Bethlehem, when Yassar Arafat appeared at the UN and set off riots throughout the West Bank.

In the Judean hills, occupied Bethlehem was another country. Their army vehicles drove through narrow alleyways, rifles cocked and ready expecting trouble that never came. They passed churches and stone towers, and shuttered shops.

"This is unreal," Dov commented.

Harry looked terrified.

Joe tried to read, but the ride was too bumpy. Although it was not accepted army garb, he'd brought the coat with him from home for the cold nights. He used it as a blanket and stored his book in it.

They were stationed in the Imperial Hotel, requisitioned by the army, The conditions were great, compared to the desert hole they had come from, and to which they were to return days later. There was hot water in the showers and the food was good, but the job they were given to do was disturbing. The obsequious Arabs serving them in that hotel had been checked for security, many were Christians, but those outside glared hatred at them.

The soldiers were sent to stand, in riot gear, across from a Palestinian girls' school where a few dozen schoolgirls, who looked no more than fourteen years old, were demonstrating their support for Arafat. The girls were chanting in Arabic, which Joe didn't understand, but he heard the word "Nazi" chanted, and "go home" yelled at them in English. Suddenly a rock came flying out at the soldiers from the back of the crowd. No one was hit. The officer yelled out an order, and they lobbed tear gas canisters into the crowd. Joe heard screams as the girls were forcefully dispersed, saw a bleeding girl being accompanied to a Red Crescent ambulance, waiting nearby.

He felt humiliated by all of this, and didn't see the sense of it, so after one round of standing with his baton and rubber bullets and trying to look tough, he begged off. He went to the medic on duty with his injured leg (he had twisted it in training a couple of days earlier) and exaggerated the symptoms and the limp. The young guy was probably no more than nineteen, while Joe was already twenty-five, an experienced "man of the world"! It wasn't hard to convince the inexperienced medic that he was in great pain.

"You've badly sprained your ankle, maybe broken it," he commented, as he bandaged the leg.

"Yeah, it's very painful to walk on. Can you give me a painkiller, so I'm able to do my duty?"

"I'll do better than that. I'll send you to the company doctor. I think we should have it x-rayed. Meanwhile, you should stay off it as much as possible."

It was x-rayed the next day. There was no break, not even the slightest fracture, but the doctor winked at him and agreed that he needed to rest the foot as it was badly bruised. With his paper in hand, giving him an exemption from physical exertion, he limped demonstratively back to the waiting jeep that had delivered him to the army regional medical clinic.

The driver, Charlie's friend, sat there smoking and looking bored. Charlie, whom he had bumped into earlier in the corridor of that decaying Bethlehem hotel, was helpful in arranging this, though he was disapproving and maybe suspected that Joe was acting up to get a break from duty.

"You need to toughen up a bit more," Charlie had commented. "And don't be so soft on the Arabs, they only respect force, you know."

Joe understood from their brief conversation in the hotel corridor that he should keep his doubts to himself.

Joe was glad to get back to their desert base after that. Two weeks later they rehearsed an attack against a fortified position. Joe was placed at the end of the second line of attack next to Fred, a guy from Dallas, Texas, who barely knew any Hebrew. The lieutenant emphasized that they were to open fire only after he gave the order and they had repeated it aloud. They carried out a couple of successful dry runs and then loaded their M-16s with live bullets.

Joe felt the sweat running down his back as they waited to run out. He knew this was a dangerous exercise.

The officer yelled something, but Joe, who was on the extreme left of the group and couldn't hear, kept running forward, as had the Texan to his right in the attacking line. A moment later bullets started flying past them and they dived to the ground.

The officer screamed out "Cease fire! Halt!" at the top of his lungs, "safety locks on!" He called all the soldiers back, made them assemble before him and, white in the face, told them that the exercise was now cancelled.

"Those two," he said pointing to Fred and Joe, "are lucky to be alive!"

Joe almost fainted on hearing this, the Texan started laughing.

"Shut up," the platoon sergeant screamed.

Now, turning to them, the lieutenant asked them: "Do you know what "Birkat Hagomel" is?"

"No," Joe mumbled.

The Texan stood there smiling stupidly and shaking his head.

"Well, you should find out. Go say you're grateful to be alive in the morning prayer minyan tomorrow."

Joe dutifully did so the next morning, Dov accompanying him. One of the religious soldiers showed them how to put on tefillin and handed them each a prayer book. He was called to the Torah and recited the blessing: "Blessed are You, Lord our God, ruler of the world, who rewards the undeserving with goodness, and who has rewarded me with goodness." The other worshippers all knew why Joe was there that morning. They answered "Amen!" with feeling.

Fred went on sleeping.

A week later a letter arrived for Joe. It was addressed to "Corporal Joe Kamens", Nahal, Army Post 3531, I.D.F.

He opened it and found a note inside with the now familiar handwriting:

Dear Yossi,
I heard about the training accident.
Thank God you are alive! Take care of yourself.
Joseph Borowski
p.s. I will contact you when I am able to."

He read the letter a second time, then remembered to look at the envelope. Picking it up, he saw the army address on the back.

This time I have an address! Bora knows where I am in the army!? He knows about the training accident! How? He must be in contact with my officers. He's never left me a way to contact him before. Rivka, Gershon... they told me they didn't know where he is, but... at last, I have a lead... he's slipped up this time. And why this "Thank God, you're alive!" stuff?

He felt his head exploding. So many questions, he told himself to calm down, but kept obsessing... I've got to write to him right away!

He wrote a note and sent it to that army address, but never received a response. Weeks, then months, passed with no further sign of life from Bora.

He received a letter from his parents. They planned to visit in about a month, wrote that they missed him, and thought it was time to visit. Would that work for him?

He wrote back that the timing of their visit was OK for him, as he would then be back on the kibbutz for his "shalat", his off-duty kibbutz period, that he looked forward to seeing them.

"By the way," he added, "I have heard from Bora!"

Chapter 16

LOVE AND MARRIAGE

Going home from the army one time Joe and Jenny rendezvoused at the desolate Tzemach intersection. One car from Kibbutz Ein Gev stopped to pick up the two other soldiers waiting with them, and then nothing stopped. They were stuck there alone a long time, watching as trucks and buses passed, leaving them standing, frustrated and tired at the dusty bus stop.

During their hours' long wait there, they got to talking: "So, tell me more about your childhood in Melbourne, Joe. What was it like having Holocaust survivors as parents?"

"Not much to tell, Jen. They didn't share much, mainly kept their bad memories to themselves."

"What, nothing?"

"I... overheard things. Almost all their friends were survivors. They talked among themselves..."

"Like what?"

Her eyes shone with interest, and empathy he couldn't resist, so he tried to open up to her: "They were from Warsaw, both lost their entire families in the ghetto, and Treblinka. I grew up with no other family – no grandparents, no uncles or aunts, no cousins, no one."

"Sounds hard. How about your friends, were they the same?"

"Yeah. Most of them. That was normal for us. Some had maybe one uncle or aunt, not more. There were other survivors living nearby, some of them were friendly, kind of. I had an "Aunt Betty" who my mum spent time with, someone she befriended on the ship, but she wasn't really family. I didn't like Mrs. Ruben much. My dad had a guy he would drink with who'd been in the D.P. camp in Germany with him, but they mostly met at a pub, not at our home."

"Hmm, it sounds depressing, intense..."

"I guess it was, don't know."

Joe held back tears. He'd forgotten to mention his youth

movement friends, Judy and the rest, whom he'd learned to love like family. He'd never thought about his childhood this way. Jenny took his hand. They stood there silently looking into each other's eyes. She kissed him, but he couldn't cry, not even for her. He hugged her instead, feeling her body respond to his.

It was dark when Shimon pulled over and invited them into the kibbutz van. Joe looked at his watch. They'd been there four hours, but he had lost his sense of time. They were still holding hands in the van as silent Shimon slowly drove up the dark snake path. Shimon asked no questions, but Joe saw his look when they got in, and his glances in the mirror. Shimon understood.

Joe's heart was thumping that entire journey.

■■■

Joe's parents' visit was impending. He'd finished his army training and was back on the kibbutz. He and Jenny were now sleeping together. She moved into his room when he got back from his last active military duty, exiling Dov to another.

It was "hot and heavy". They were necking all the time, kissing in public, walking around holding hands, and not sleeping much. He was back in the bananas, she went back to working in the moadon, but had a new second job as well.

He hadn't told his parents about her, but now that they would soon be arriving, he thought it might be best to say something, to write or phone and tell them he had a girlfriend. He didn't understand why he kept putting off doing so.

Jenny became a medic in the army and was so good at it that her commander put her in charge of a small army clinic. When she got out of the army, the kibbutz work coordinator asked her to go back to running the moadon. She agreed but asked to spend time helping in the kibbutz clinic as well. She started doing that a couple of mornings a week. The kibbutz members appreciated her there, praised her for her serious approach, her conscientiousness, and her gentle touch.

Joe loved her touch, understood why people at the clinic mentioned it. Jenny's presence was soothing, calming. He loved her, but... He imagined she would be a good mother one day, but... she could be so naive in some ways.

Now that his parents were coming, he had to decide how serious he was about their relationship.

He loved so many things about her. Jenny was lively, pretty and kind. She was his closest friend. Her boundless cheerfulness was wonderful, though sometimes when he was in one of his dark moods, it bugged him. She often had a good, optimistic word to put in about anything negative or critical he said, but she didn't see the dark side of things that he perceived in the army, in the kibbutz, and in Israeli society.

The kibbutz members had little understanding or respect for the rights of others, of Arabs, of Mizrahi Jews, of new immigrants. Like in the army, the kibbutz was dominated by a harsh view of the world that valued toughness and looked down on the "misfits", the weak. The longer he was in the country, the more he perceived a gap between what they'd been told about the country and its reality.

The kibbutz communal meetings were concerned with self-interest, material benefits, and profits, not issues of social justice. He participated as often as he could, listening at meeting after meeting as they discussed having a TV in every home and rejected potential members when their candidacy was put to a vote because they weren't popular enough, or happened to be "the wrong kind of person for us". Just as in the army he'd seen profound class divisions and callousness, so too he experienced it in the kibbutz. It seemed more like a closed social club for former warriors than the socialist utopia that he'd envisioned. In the army, who you knew was more important than who you were, a phone call from the right connection solved problems there, and on the kibbutz, it was the same.

But Jenny saw none of that.

He talked to her about his doubts, his disappointments with the kibbutz, about his growing disillusionment with the country and its treatment of the poor, of minorities. He shared critical and disturbing newspaper articles with her. He told her about the structure of discrimination between Jews and Arabs built into the courts, the police, and other institutions of the country, the political corruption.

Jenny listened but remained impervious. She shrugged off such things as the words of angry, bitter old men.

"Ben Gurion was smart"; "Everything will work itself out for the best"; "No worries, mate!" she would say, using the expression she'd learned from the Aussies who visited him, like Charlie, who loved that phrase.

"Anyway, the Arabs are our enemy," she'd add.

Maybe it was her infectious optimism that attracted him to her as she countered his negative musings, but it grated sometimes, was overwhelming sometimes. But despite all that, he knew he loved her, and that she loved him.

One evening when Jenny had finished her evening shift, they went for a stroll along the path at the western edge of the kibbutz, just below the moadon. The panoramic view of the Kinneret lake below, the distant twinkling lights of the city of Tiberias on the lower left edge of the water, the clear starlit sky above them with its sliver of the honey-coloured moon were a serene and romantic backdrop to their conversation, but they were not at peace with each other.

Joe reminded Jenny of his parents' upcoming visit, but then he started talking about Bora, that he was determined to find the man, wanted to know more about him now that he knew he was still alive and in the country. She listened, walking along beside him holding his arm. Joe felt her tense up as he spoke. Suddenly, she let go of his arm, stopped walking, and glared angrily at him.

"I'm sick of hearing about Bora, Joe. It's become an obsession of yours! I want to talk about us, and want to know where I stand before your parents show up here."

"But Jenny… Don't get so upset. Bora holds the key to my understanding of who I am."

"I don't get what you are talking about, Joe. You don't need to talk to him to know who you are! I know who you are. The past doesn't matter. It's long dead. Gone. Finished. Over!"

"I'm sorry, Jen, but that doesn't work for me. I've got to know what the story is, what happened in the past to understand the present."

"Joe, you are impossible! Why don't you try meditating, or reading more positive stuff? I have a great book on Yoga philosophy I could lend you. I could show you breathing exercises that would help you learn how to relax..."

"Listen to me, Jenny. Calm down. I'm not into that spiritual stuff you do. It's not for me. You know that. Let me explain about Bora..."

"Explain what! The past...? That you can't let go of it...? I see what you're reading all the time. It's all terrible, depressing, heavy stuff. You spend your spare time reading about starving people, mass murder, genocide, war, revenge, concentration camps, politics... It's too much, Joe, pulling you down all the time... and that old coat... I think you should throw it away."

She turned away from him, started walking back towards the moadon. He followed her, called after her. She was upset, so was he. Her criticism hurt him, but he thought he understood her, wanted to make up with her. He wanted her to understand how important these things were to him, especially his need to find Bora.

As they approached the darkened moadon building, they heard voices coming from inside, saw a flickering blue light inside. When they entered the room, they found a small crowd, sitting facing the television set, listening. Jenny had walked in angry, Joe following, self-conscious and awkward. He saw some of his friends look up in his direction with questioning eyes.

This is a news flash!

The round-faced, bespectacled man in the TV was speaking:

There has been a dramatic political development...

Joe watched, standing at the back. Jenny sat down next to Dov and Harry, who didn't notice her at first. Joe sat down next to her. She moved away, sat at the other end of the row, on the other side of Harry. Dov looked over at him with a knowing smile. Joe ignored it.

The Agranat Commission presented its interim report last week. It cleared Moshe Dayan of responsibility for the lack of preparedness of the army for the Yom Kippur War. Despite that, the public protest calling for his resignation has continued and grown in numbers. Thousands have taken to the streets...

"We know all that already," Harry grumbled. "When will he get to the point?"

"Shush!" said an annoyed woman in the front row, turning back with her finger to her lips.

Today in a Labour Party caucus meeting, Prime Minister Golda Meir announced her determination to resign forthwith from political life, only one month after forming the country's 16th government. She told the party leadership this evening: "I have reached the end of the road. I cannot carry on any longer." The political system is in turmoil because of this sudden surprising announcement...

Everyone in the room started talking at once, arguing about who should replace Golda, causing pandemonium in the moadon.

In the middle of all this, Jenny got up and left the room. Dov gave Joe a poke.

"What's going on, Joey?"

"Yeah. What's up?" Harry asked.

"Nothing guys. Nothing. She's just nervous because my parents are coming."

"Why? Are you two going to announce something? It's about time."

"No. I'm not ready to make that kind of commitment yet."

The next day Jenny moved back into her old room. Joe was stunned. He thought it had only been a minor argument. But now that she was gone, he felt despondent. He came back from work to an empty room. Her scent was still there, he still found her hair in his bathroom. She'd left behind a couple of books about meditation and her yoga rug. He realized just how much he loved her, that he couldn't live without her.

His friends advised him to keep his cool, that this fight would pass, that she would come back to him sooner or later. But that didn't happen. Two long bleak days passed without contact. He phoned and discussed his malaise with Rivka.

"Do you love her, Yossi?"

"Yes, I do."

"Well then, go tell her so."

But Jenny was avoiding Joe. He didn't know what to do. He saw her sitting there in the dining hall with the other young women, happily chatting. Whenever he looked her way, tried to make eye-contact with her, she looked away, gave him no hint of invitation, or even recognition. It was painful, frustrating, and now he knew that he wanted to marry her, that he had to do something radical.

On the evening of the third day, he went over to her room, carrying her books, the yoga rug, and a ring. He knocked on the door.

"Who's there?"

"It's me." He put the rug and books down and took out the ring in preparation.

"Go away!"

"Listen, Jenny, I've got something to give you. You left stuff behind in my room. And we must talk. We can't go on like this…"

The door opened. He stood facing her, holding his gift out. Jenny's eyes were red. She looked down at the little red-maroon box in his hand. He opened it to show her.

"Will you marry me?"

"Oh, Joe!"

She was crying. He took the ring out and put it on the middle finger of her left hand. She wiped away some of her tears, broke into a smile and nodded yes. He put his arms around her waist. She pulled him still closer. They kissed.

The next morning, they heard on the radio before work that Yitzhak Rabin was chosen to be the new leader of the Labour Party and was appointed Prime Minister. They both yawned and went to work.

Jenny moved back in with him. Joe started reading more widely, about eastern spiritual traditions, about meditation. He followed Jenny's instructions on breathing techniques and correct posture for meditation. He began to do so regularly, with her.

New elections were announced.

Then his parents arrived.

Eva came up to the kibbutz with Rivka. Joe stood there in his warm partisan coat watching as a blue rented Volkswagen drove up. He saw two women inside and recognized them at once but what had become of his father?

Rivka, tall and graceful as always, got out of the car from the driver's side, then Eva emerged. Beside Rivka his stooped mother looked diminutive and grey. Rivka opened the baggage compartment and pulled out two coats for protection against the chilly afternoon wind. They put them on and approached smiling.

He was smiling too.

"Hello Yossi. It's wonderful to see you!"

"Hi Mum."

"You're still wearing that old coat."

"Yes…"

"You look tired…"

Joe frowned, but his frown melted when his mother kissed him, and he was joyfully hugged by Rivka.

"Where's Dad?" he asked, as the two women stood looking around them. "And Lily?"

"Yanosh stayed in the hotel in Tiberias and Lily decided to stay with him. He asked us to pick you up and drive you down to the hotel."

"He's still upset about me being in the Golan!? Is that why he didn't come up here with you?"

"You know your father…"

"Shalom Yossi! It's good to see you again. I am so sorry we couldn't manage to visit you in the army on Parents' Day. We couldn't get the kibbutz car. Motti sends his love. Did you receive my letters? We were worried about you."

"Yes, I got them and yours, Mum…"

"I worry about you, darling. I know army life can be rough. You're a suburban kid… not prepared for country life either. You do look good though, I admit… not like in the picture you sent us. You were so thin there. I see you've put on some weight again. Kibbutz life agrees with you, yes?"

"Yes, it does... Follow me."

"Lead the way, Joey!"

Joe started walking along the gravel path towards the only apparent communal building in sight. Eva and Rivka followed, arm in arm, looking around at the barren, flat area through which they were walking. Black basalt rocks skirted the path, and the beginnings of some "lawns" soon appeared, sprouting on either side in patches of brown soil. They approached a low, long, concrete prefab building, its long windows emitting the sounds of men and women talking, some arguing loudly. There were no children to be seen, but there was a row of baby carriages near one end of the building, and a couple of battered bicycles.

Joe pointed out some green saplings nearby.

"I planted those. One day they'll provide shade. Here's a grape vine, and that little one over there is an olive tree."

"Wonderful!" Rivka exclaimed. "You're truly halutzim up here!"

"Very nice, Joey. Very nice, but it's so isolated... So far away."

"Far away from where?"

"From your home... from your family... from Melbourne," Eva replied.

Her wrinkled brow told Joe all he needed to know.

Rivka laughed. "Yes, and far away from us old kibbutzniks as well!"

"She's right. Far away from Rivka and Motti too! They were kind enough to provide a home away from home for you. Who do you have up here to care for you!?"

Joe didn't know what to say in response. They didn't know about Jenny yet. He saw the concern in his mother's eyes. She looked old.

"This is our dining hall," he explained, opening the door.

As they climbed the few steps up to the open dining hall door, Joe pointed out another, smaller, building below them. Beyond it they could see a wire fence skirting around a circular grey path along a cliff edge, and just beneath that a view of the

Sea of Galilee.

"That's our members' moadon, and there's the Kinneret," Joe said, pointing.

"It's cold standing out here in the wind," Eva said.

"The wind blows like this every afternoon here. We'll go inside. After you rest up a bit, I'll take you down to the moadon, and introduce you to Jenny."

"Who's Jenny?" Eva asked.

"Your girlfriend!" Rivka guessed.

"Mum! Rivka! Wait a minute. Come inside first. Later, I'll answer your questions..."

After a short warm up in the dining hall, Joe led his mother and Rivka down to the moadon.

"Hi, Jenny! We're here!" he called out, as they came up to the door of the little concrete building. They heard a woman singing inside.

"I'll be right there in a moment!" a voice chirped from inside.

Joe recognized the tune, "Sunrise, sunset..." the song from the wedding scene in "Fiddler on the Roof".

He laughed to himself. Rivka noticed that and gave him a questioning look. Eva didn't notice.

They walked into a medium-sized room furnished with low tables and cushioned chairs, facing a panoramic view of the lake below. A short pretty woman in jeans and t-shirt wearing a colourful apron over her front looked up at them from whatever she was doing in a kitchenette corner space.

Jenny stopped singing when they walked in, greeting them with a warm smile.

"Jenny, meet my mum, and her friend Rivka."

"Hello." Jenny's smile broadened, her eyes alight with joy. "Nice to meet you..."

"Shalom, Mrs. Kamens, and Rivka! Joe has told me so much about both of you."

Eva and Rivka stood there, wordless. Eva's wrinkles deepened as she surveyed the young woman, Jenny's smile disappeared. Rivka put her hand gently on Eva's shoulder.

Joe suggested that they sit down. "Over here... for coffee.

I'll put the kettle on..."

They sat down at one of the tables, Rivka commenting on the beautiful view, Eva nodding in appreciation. Jenny returned with a tray of hot and cold drinks. Her engagement ring glistened in a ray of light coming through the window they were facing.

Joe saw that his mother's eyes were focused on the ring.

"Haven't I told you yet? Jenny and I decided to get married."

"What!" Eva's eyes turned away from the view to look at the young couple. They were now wide open.

"What a surprise!" Rivka said without looking surprised at all, again placing her hand on Eva's shoulder. Eva visibly relaxed and managed a smile.

"Jenny, forgive me. It's just the shock of it all. We only just met... Joe, why didn't you tell us anything? That's good news. Mazel Tov! When and where are you planning to have the wedding? Perhaps we can do it in Melbourne?"

"No, Mum, not there, but since you and dad are here, and Lily too... It's so far to come especially from Australia again... and so expensive..."

"What are you saying?" Eva asked, her forehead again wrinkled.

"We decided to surprise you and do the ceremony in the rabbinical offices in Tiberias next week... on Tuesday afternoon. You and Motti will come, I hope."

"Of course, we will."

"Next week?" Eva asked, her voice strained.

"Yep. You'll still be in the country, right?"

"And what about a party? Your father won't be happy about all this suddenness, you know."

"Well, dad doesn't like big parties, neither do I. I know dad's issue with the territories. We booked a restaurant in Tiberias; we'll be nearby for that evening."

Eva turned to her friend, having pushed her hand off her shoulder: "Rivka, you don't look shocked at all this. You knew?"

"Not exactly, Eva. He didn't talk to me about it, but I understood something's cooking. Motti and I have seen them together, and they did tell us to keep that date free."

Joe had taken Jenny's hand. They sat there looking at Eva, smiling expectantly.

"Well. We'll have to change our plans. This is so unexpected," Eva mumbled.

"Mazal Tov! You two look so happy together. Motti will be delighted, he thought you were a good match. Eva, are you all right?"

"Just in shock. A little headache… Uhh… we must phone Yanosh and inform him."

"Wait a minute. I'll get you something to drink."

Joe winked at Jenny and Rivka.

He returned with some shot glasses and a bottle of yellow liquid.

"I know you like white wine, Mum. Let's drink leHaim!"

Then they went to the dining room to call Yanosh.

On the way, Joe took his mother's arm.

"Mum, there is something else I haven't told you."

"More surprises?"

"Well, yes. You see while I was in the army, during training in the Negev, there was an incident, a training accident."

Eva turned around to look at him directly, a worried look in her eyes.

"It's OK, Mum. Nothing really happened. No one was hurt, but soon afterwards I received a letter from your old friend, Bora."

"Bora?" She let go of her son's arm, tensed up, but continued walking.

"Yes. He'd heard of the accident in the army somehow and tried to make contact, promised to call again but I haven't heard from him since."

"Strange. Listen, Joe. Bora is no friend of mine, and you should stay away from him. Bora means trouble. I heard he was alive and still doing mischief of some kind over here. I want you to avoid the man as much as you can. And please don't mention any of this to your father, OK?"

Rivka took Eva's arm but said nothing.

"Whatever you say," Joe responded.

They went into the dining hall, waited for the phone to be free, and called Yanosh.

Joe was unhappy that his father had not come up to the kibbutz and saddened by his mother's unenthusiastic reaction to their announcement of marriage plans. As he and Jenny drove down to the hotel in Tiberias to meet Yanosh and Lily, Joe's mind flashed back to traumatic past events in his family life.

His relationship with his father had never been an easy one, nor had his parents' marriage. He saw the image of his father smashing plates in their kitchen, remembered his mother standing there crying, and his own childish impotence at the time. He remembered his father's disappearances, the days of angry silence...

He pulled the car over to the side of the road before they started their descent on the snake path, rubbed his watery eyes.

"What's the matter, Joe?"

"I want you to drive. I'm finding it hard to concentrate. I guess I'm upset."

"About what? I thought the first meeting with your mother went well."

"I'm not so sure. Rivka was great. She was very sweet, but my mum... she reacted strangely."

"Really... I suppose... you know your mother..."

"And my dad's reaction on the phone was... eh... he was angry. Didn't you see how my mother and Rivka left suddenly? They didn't even stay to look around the kibbutz at all before leaving. They were in such a hurry to go."

"I think you're upsetting yourself unnecessarily. Your mother was a little taken by surprise, that's all. She wanted you to share the news in person with your father and sister. That's not so surprising, and they knew you needed to arrange a car for us so we could return to the kibbutz this evening. That's why they left us, to arrange things: they hurried to drive down before dark. Didn't she say they would also try to arrange a room for us in the hotel? That's very kind."

"Maybe, but… listen, Jenny, there are things I haven't told you about my father and my relationship with him… I think I should do that now on the way, before you meet him. I want you to understand, to be prepared."

"Now you are making me nervous."

"It'll be all right. But drive slowly."

"Yes, I think we'd better start moving again, sweetheart. They're waiting for us. Try to relax and stay calm."

She reached over and kissed him. He returned the kiss, stroked her hair, smiled, and then closed his eyes. He concentrated on deep breathing for a while. She continued driving. Tears rolled down Joe's cheeks.

"So… I don't get on well with my dad."

"What do you mean?"

"He's a difficult, stubborn person. Everything is a matter of principle with him."

"I know. You've told me that before."

"Yeah, but what I haven't told you is that he has violent outbursts… and that my mother threatened to leave him a few times over the years."

"It must have been rough for you as a kid."

Joe nodded.

Chapter 17

THE WEDDING

The wedding was a modest one. There was the rabbi and his assistant with their beards, ritual fringes, and black suits. Joe wore black slacks and a purple shirt, Jenny wore an off-white semi-formal dress, decorated with blue lace flowers around the back, and blue trimming around the front. She covered her hair with a light white transparent scarf. He wore a small, sky-blue kippa. The guests were informally dressed.

His parents and Lily were there, of course.

Rivka and Motti were there, and their friends, fellow soldiers from Kibbutz Afikei Kinneret, Dov and Harry, and Steve, and Selma.

Steve just happened to be visiting his friends in Israel at the time. Two days earlier, Joe had called him at his hotel in Tel Aviv when he heard he was in the country.

"Jenny? You're marrying Jenny!"

"Yes, the pretty girl who used to run the moadon. You remember her, don't you? The petite one with the auburn hair and sunny personality, who was doing yoga all the time on the kibbutz lawn. You introduced us."

"Oh, yes, I did. That's right. I thought you two would make a great match. I guess I got that one right... Anyway, Mazel Tov, Joe! That's great news!"

"And you'll come up north for our wedding?"

"Of course, I wouldn't miss it."

Nicky, the poet, was there. He read a poem he had written in honour of the occasion.

Charlie came from the army, despite the short notice, but said he had to leave right after the ceremony. He came in, with a large green kippa covering his forehead, tzitzit – the ritual fringes – hanging out from the waistline of his uniform pants, covered in dust, and smiling from ear to ear. Joe and he hugged. A couple of other guys with whom Joe had worked in the bananas also showed up. They all, except Charlie, donned the

132

same white hotel-stamped kippas that the rabbi had supplied.

They assembled in the courtyard of the Tiberias rabbinic offices. The sun was low in the late afternoon sky. The huppa, a canopy of black and white cloth with fringes tied to four poles, was spread out over the nervous bride and groom, symbolizing their new home together. The rabbi spoke briefly to the couple before beginning the ceremony.

Joe gave Jenny the ring, after Charlie, his best man, passed it to him. He said the words the rabbi dictated to him, *"Harei at mekudeshet li beTabaat zo kedaat Moshe veYisrael... –* You are betrothed unto me with this ring according to the law of Moses and Israel." They sipped the sweet red wine, looking intensely at each other and, to end the ceremony, Joe broke the glass by stomping on it, declaring "If I forget thee Oh Jerusalem…"

Now that the couple was officially married, and more relaxed, they and their guests left to go to the Moroccan restaurant they had chosen for their festive dinner. Charlie hugged Joe and Jenny, and then headed back to his army unit.

Yanosh had refused to wear a kippa, nor did he smile during the entire wedding ceremony. But now as they walked to the restaurant, he seemed to lighten up. Joe was happy to see that his father and sister had taken a liking to Jenny.

Yanosh, Jenny and bespectacled Lily were happily chatting on the way to the restaurant followed by Eva, who walked beside Rivka, who was singing the wedding song *"Od Yishama BeArei Yehuda uvehutzot Yerushalayim –* The voices of bride and groom will yet be heard in the cities of Judea and the courtyards of Jerusalem."

They laughed at a joke Lily told them, and were all smiling as they walked along together.

Joe walked along behind them with Motti and Dov, one on either side. They were humming the same tune as the ladies while their little procession progressed along the rough asphalt path towards the restaurant.

The "Rambam" fish restaurant was just off Hagalil Street, near the corner of Achva Road. A waiter escorted them into a decorated back room, complete with chandeliers and gold-trimmed maroon curtains. Inside stood a long table, a white tablecloth spread over it, loaded with delicacies. A waiter produced two flower-adorned chairs that he placed at the head of the table for the bride and groom. Once they were all seated Yanosh stood up, holding a glass of vodka and proposed a toast to the young couple:

"Here's to Joe and Jenny! Wishing you both many good years together as you build your nest."

Eva rose and added: "A good Jewish home!"

"LeHaim! To Life!" Rivka joined, standing, her glass uplifted.

"LeHaim!" Motti added, standing, too, their other friends adding their voices to the joyous chorus.

They sat down to begin the meal which Joe enjoyed, but Jenny barely ate anything.

Later, after everyone had left, Joe overheard his parents' angry conversation in the hotel corridor: "I want you to come up to the kibbutz to see where your son and your daughter-in-law live. It's beautiful there, an incredible view."

"I'm sorry, Eva. I'm not going to do that. Settling civilians in an area conquered in war is against international law, against the Geneva Convention."

"You're so stubborn. Not everything is politics!"

Then the door closed behind them as they entered their neighbouring room. He and Jenny could hear them yelling in the next room but could no longer hear their words clearly. They heard something crash. Then there was silence.

"What's going on in there, Joe? Your parents sound like alley cats fighting."

They've stopped now. They do that all the time, but they make up. They'll be cheerful at breakfast tomorrow morning.

Joe winked at Jenny suggestively. They cuddled.

"Maybe then you can talk to your father, get him to change his mind and come up to the kibbutz."

"Maybe."

But Yanosh never visited the kibbutz.

They all met again for a day at Rivka's kibbutz and a trip to the sea before finally saying goodbye at Lod airport. Joe's parents returned to Australia with a parting wish to see the young couple next in Melbourne. Yanosh promised to pay their fare if they agreed to leave the kibbutz. Joe refused. He and Jenny hugged his parents and his sister. Eva and Lily cried, Yanosh, stony, unsmiling, stuffed a wad of bills in Joe's coat pocket and turned to go. Eva lingered and then joined Yanosh and Lily walking away. Joe felt sad, but was happy to see them go.

I'll come when I can buy the ticket myself, but I'm not leaving the kibbutz so I don't know if I'll ever see them again.

As they left the terminal, Jenny said: "I'd love to visit them in Australia, but not yet."

"Someday," Joe answered, finding it hard to speak.

■■■

A week after the wedding, a postcard arrived from Vienna for Joe and Jenny:

Mazal Tov to the young couple!
I am sorry I could not join you for your joyous occasion as I was overseas. I will come to visit next opportunity.
Joseph Borowski

Joe was spooked by this. He told Jenny, but she smiled kindly and said she thought he should relax, that what would be, would be. But he couldn't relax. He was obsessing:

How did Bora know about our wedding? Why is he sending greetings from overseas? When will he visit? Why? I'm tired of this cat and mouse game with him. These messages out of the blue are unnerving. What is he, some kind of spy or assassin or something?

Joe called Rivka to talk, to tell her he'd heard from Bora again, to complain about his strange behaviour. Joe trusted Rivka's wisdom, found her voice on the phone reassuring whenever they spoke. She told him she'd talk to Motti, that maybe he knew something about how to contact Bora. She hadn't spoken to Bora since Joe left her kibbutz, and didn't know where he was, but Motti had friends who worked with him, who might know something.

Rivka called back the next evening to say that Motti couldn't tell her much, except to advise that he have a little more patience. He told her that he'd heard rumours about Bora, that he might be retiring soon and would be around more, that there was some kind of personal tragedy. Rivka added that she didn't think it a good idea to rely on rumours.

Joe hadn't thought to invite this mysterious man he'd never met in any case. It would have been a problem as they'd understood from Eva. They'd kept his father out of the picture regarding Bora. He decided he should give up his search for him.

But Bora kept re-emerging in his life, uninvited.

Chapter 18
BACK TO THE ARMY

A couple of months went by in work and love. Joe and Jenny settled into married life, forgetting the army would call him back to active service, but the day came.

Selma brought them both letters that same day.

"You haven't been to collect your mail in a few days, you young lovers," she said laughing. "These were burning a hole on my desk, so I decided to deliver them personally."

Joe's heart fell when he saw the brown envelopes with their army insignia in her hand. He knew what it was right away before Selma handed them over.

"I'm out of the army!" Jenny exclaimed after ripping open hers.

Selma hugged her.

They looked over at Joe as he hesitated and then opened his:

"Joe, you look like someone died," Selma commented.

"I have to go back, and they're not sending me back to my unit but down to Sinai. Awful news."

"But that's so far away." Jenny's joyful expression had disappeared.

"Too far. I'm going to argue with them, until they let me go back to my Nahal unit." He said that with determination, but he knew army bureaucracy." *It's not going to be easy.*

"Joe, I'll miss you." Jenny put her arm around his waist, gripping him as if she wanted to keep him there, not let him go.

He bent down and kissed her, but remained silent, caught up in his angry thoughts about the army, remembering the bad food, the smell of gunpowder and the lack of sleep.

I hate the bloody army. I should be here with Jenny.

■■■

But Joe had to go, however reluctant he felt. And he didn't know what awaited him.

It was a long journey through a barren land. He travelled

with soldiers he'd never met before.

Hot in his army uniform, boots, and jacket, he and the other guys in the back of the truck began to strip off as much as they could, and drank water. They were swimming in sweat, wiping their brows with strips of cloth they'd torn off a roll of material normally used to clean oil off their weapons. One of them noticed his ring.

"Married?" he asked.

"Yes."

"What are you doing here?"

"Long story," he answered.

He looked at the hot, greasy faces of the other men and wondered what their stories were. He'd been transferred to a different unit because he'd received a postponement.

He thought of Jenny and how happy they'd been until the army called him back. He pulled her photo out of his pocket to show the other guys, but they were dozing. He glanced at her beaming face once again and then put it back.

My wife, Jenny... I'm still not used to that...

I hope she's OK and doesn't worry about me too much. She looked devastated when I left. Always cheerful and resilient but she looked so small and vulnerable. I should be there with her, not here!

He remembered how he'd reported to the Nahal head offices in Jaffo to arrange the deferment, the frustration of trying to reconnect with his unit, which was serving in the tank corps in Sinai. The commanding officer promised him it could be arranged, but that didn't happen.

After three months on the kibbutz – and a round of exasperating phone calls – the officer on the phone angrily told him to report again without further argument, and there he was served his order to go down to the Sinai. He wasn't being sent to his own unit after all. He'd argued with the officer who had issued that order, but to no avail.

The guy, whose pinched face was covered with acne scars and whose hair was thinning, promised him that he would eventually be able to rejoin his unit. For the time being he would just have to do what he was told and report to another unit. As he bounced up and down in the army truck recalling that conversation, he remembered the sound of the officer's impatient tapping on that desk in Jaffo.

"At least you will be nearby, and not up north," that ugly lieutenant had told him. He had wondered whether that was a cynical comment. The thought had crossed his mind that "up north" would have been better, but his new status as a married soldier made no impression on the man. He was more impressed with the record of repeated requests to go down to Sinai.

"No arguments any longer! Just go! That's an order," the man yelled at him. He could tell the guy was bored and uninterested, that his "anger" was a performance. But there was nothing more he could do.

Despite the heat, the noise, and the discomfort in the back of the truck, all four soldiers fell asleep after a while. Joe thought of Jenny and the growing distance between them. He would try to talk to his officers in this new unit to get himself transferred north. Listening to the other men snore and the rhythmic sound of rifles and army boots hitting the wooden ammunition crates across which they had spread themselves, he could no longer keep his eyes open.

When they came to a stop at a fence of barbed wire along a row of concrete blocks, he knew they had reached the bunkers of the southernmost defence line opposite the Egyptians… the line to which the army had withdrawn after ceasefire negotiations.

Two weeks passed in the Sinai army installation. He read poems by David Avidan, sketched faces of the men around him, played chess a couple of times a day with his new Yemenite friend, Eliezer, and heard jokes about prostitutes in Tel Aviv, football, and the stock exchange; but he hadn't pinned down the officer-in-charge to talk about a transfer.

The jeep drove into their military outpost, amid a cloud of dust and sand, once every couple of days. He made a point of greeting the red-faced inspecting captain. The man's blue eyes looked at him blankly at first, until, with time, the man began to recognize him. His put-offs and promises were different each time, but never led to a real conversation with him.

"I know. I know, Yossi," the officer would say. "You were just married. They made some mistake. You want to transfer up north. I'm working on it."

But nothing happened.

Then on the fourteenth day, just when he was giving up hope, two letters arrived with the officer in his jeep. The captain presented them to him with a cold, ironic smile.

"This is for you, Yossi. And this one too."

Joe looked at the two envelopes. One was brown with the I.D.F. stamp on it, the other a decorated blue and white one. From Jenny! He was sure it was, though there was no address on it. He kissed it, then stowed it in his top shirt pocket, deciding to wait until he was alone to read it. The other, the brown envelope, demanded immediate attention. He ripped it open. Eliezer and the officer watched him do so, laughing.

Joe read the words in joyful disbelief. He wondered if Bora had somehow been involved in this abrupt change in his luck.

"It's my transfer! I'm to report back to the Nahal office in Jaffo by 11:00 a.m. tomorrow. But how will I ever be able to make it there on time from this hole!?"

"You'll be there on time, don't worry, Yossi," the officer said.

"That is a problem, but you'll find a way, I'm sure. Mazal tov, Yossi!" Eliezer piped in.

"I'm going to miss our chess games… and our discussions of politics." Eliezer smiled sadly.

Joe hugged him. He wanted to share his joy, but also to express his support for his new friend. He knew how hard it was to find someone else to talk to in the rough army reality of an isolated outpost. The officer had wandered off, but now returned.

"Yosef Kamens?" asked the officer.

"Yes, that's the name."

"Go get your kitbag. Throw it into the jeep. We're leaving after I talk to the local commander. Shouldn't be long. You have some high-up friend who got you out of here, so it won't be a problem."

The captain delivered Joe near midnight to the Beersheba

"Beit HeHayal" soldier's club and hostel where he slept the night. The next morning, he skipped breakfast, apart from a quick cup of coffee and headed out to the central bus station. Pushing through the crowds to the ticket window, he showed the ticket seller his soldier's card, bought a ticket to Tel Aviv, then sprinted to catch the bus. He jumped onto the bus at the last possible moment, as the doors closed.

In the Tel Aviv central bus station, he made his way through the stalls for fast-foods, drinks and cheap clothing, and dodged the street-sellers selling tapes of "Mizrahi" music, until he reached the taxi stand. There he boarded a "sherut" shuttle going south along Jerusalem Boulevard into Jaffo. It had been a long, tiring journey with no stops and nothing to eat or drink, other than the water he sipped from his army canteen, and some stale potato chips he'd found in his kitbag. Before going into the Nahal offices, he found himself a falafel kiosk and bought a pita with hummus and salad that he ate quickly, then washed it down with a cup of lemonade.

He set foot in the Nahal offices at 10:30 a.m., half an hour earlier than the set time on his orders. A miracle! He took a deep breath and sat down to catch his breath for a moment, and to think.

The girl at the reception desk let him make a phone call. He called the kibbutz dining hall number, hoping to catch Jenny there. After a couple of rings, a man's voice answered.

"Hello. Is Jenny there?"

"Yes. Just wait a moment. I'll call her."

"Joe, is that you?!"

"Hi, sweetheart. I got my transfer! I'll be home tonight."

She let out a shriek of joy.

"Joe, I've some news to share when you get here."

"What's that? Is everything all right? Did something happen?"

"No, nothing to worry about. Let's not talk about it now. Not now, darling. When you get here…"

They blew kisses and hung up. Joe wondered what Jenny had to tell him. He thought about that all the way home.

Chapter 19

HOME AGAIN

When Joe reached Tiberias, he called Jenny. "Anyone from the kibbutz down here to give me a ride home?"

"Joe! Where are you? In Tiberias?"

"Yes. If I get a ride, I can be home in a couple of hours. Can't wait!"

"I'll find out if the car is out today. Can you call me back? Give me about twenty minutes and then call the dining hall."

"Yeah, I still have some asimonim – phone tokens. I'll call back."

Twenty minutes later: "Hello, Jenny?"

"Hello, Joe! Yes. It's me. Nachshon is at the hardware shop on Rachel Street. He said he'd wait for you there."

"Great. See you soon!" Joe sprinted to meet Nachshon.

■■■

Up the snake path, past the overturned burned-out tractor, past the "Danger of Death – Land Mines" signs and then onto the higher Golan plain, with its fields of swaying golden wheat, wandering cows and abandoned Syrian army ruins. Nachshon soon was driving into the kibbutz, Joe asleep in the back of the van.

He woke as the van slowed down, and saw a flock of long-necked white birds fly over the entrance area as they drove in. Jenny was standing in the parking lot, her flowery summer dress and long auburn hair blowing towards him in the afternoon wind. He started opening the door before Nachshon had parked.

"Hey, Yossi! Careful!"

As Jenny, smiling and crying, came up to the van, Joe jumped out to meet her, bounding forward like a kangaroo into her arms. Nachshon laughed at the young lovers. He walked on past, leaving them standing there on the gravel square between two tractors, kissing.

"What was it you wouldn't tell me on the phone, Jen? I'm dying of curiosity."

"Well. Last week a man called the kibbutz looking for you. I told him you're in the army. He said he would call back."

"Strange. What was his name? What did he want?"

"He didn't say much. He said his name was Joseph Borowski."

"Bora!"

"Yes. The guy you told me so much about. Joe, calm down!"

Joe had dropped his pipe. He picked it up again and relit it.

"I wonder why he suddenly called. What does he want?" Jenny asked.

"Don't know, but he makes me nervous."

A week later, in the early evening after the afternoon wind had died down, Charlie drove into the kibbutz.

Joe heard a car arrive. He was standing on the steps of the dining hall enjoying the view of the first twinkling lights in the distance as the sun disappeared below when Charlie appeared. Joe was happy to see him but knew it would be difficult because Charlie was now much more religious. He had grown out his beard, had side curls tucked behind his ears and ritual fringes hanging over the sides of his belt and jeans.

"G'day, mate! Thought I'd drop by to say hello to an old friend now that he has a break from active duty and can be pinned down."

"Hi, Charlie. What about you? You ought to be out of the army by now, no?"

"Yeah. I just got out last week. So how does it feel, Joe?"

"How does what feel?"

"You know, to be a married man?"

"Jenny and I are happy together."

What's he getting at? Joe wondered, starting to feel uncomfortable.

"I can see that, but doesn't it cramp your style? You know, no longer a free man, and all that. You watch, the next thing you know she'll be wanting to have a baby."

Charlie's smile told Joe he was being teased. The old Charlie, despite his changed appearance... he thought.

"That's cool with me. In fact, isn't that just what you should be thinking about yourself? Getting married, starting a family with lots of little religious kids," Joe said, laughing.

"That's the reason I'm here, Joey. Here take this and read."

Charlie handed him a decorative envelope. Joe opened it and pulled out the card, lighting up and smiling as he read it.

"Charlie, that's great news! Mazal Tov!"

He strode over to his old friend and hugged him, noticing the holster on Charlie's hip.

Oh, no! He is one of those settler cowboys now?

"Come on... We'll tell Jenny!" Joe said, as he manoeuvred his friend towards the moadon, "and tell me about your fiancé."

"I'll do better than that. Tamar'll be here soon... She's just parking the car and then she'll meet us in the moadon. Everyone knows how much you love the view, and that Jenny works there."

As they walked down together, Jenny appeared at the moadon door. She stood looking at them as they approached, her hands on her hips, her face full of questions.

She's beautiful when she stands there like that, framed by the door, with her hair catching the last rays of the setting sun.

"Hi, sweetheart. Guess what, we have visitors!"

"Hi, Charlie! Nice to see you."

"Shalom, Jenny. I've news. I want you to meet someone very important to me. She'll be here soon."

"Oh?"

"By the way, I don't go by that goyische name anymore. You should call me Hanoch. The name Hanoch captured my imagination. You know, it says 'he walked with God'."

He's really one of them...

"Here she is!" Charlie-Hanoch announced.

A tall, slender woman approached the moadon walking gracefully in a long dress and sandals. She wore no makeup, nor any jewellery, but her glassy blue eyes said it all. Joe saw the look of a person who had "got religion"; he braced himself for what was to come.

"Meet my fiancé, Tamar."

"Shalom Aleichem, Yossi! Shalom Aleichem, Jenny. You don't have a Hebrew name?"

Looking up at the woman, Jenny shook her head.

She's a giant. Jenny looks so small next to her.

"I have heard so much about you two. I'm honoured to finally meet you, Be'ezrat Hashem. What a miracle that all these Jewish souls have returned to Eretz Israel and found their bashert here!"

"Their what?"

"It's Yiddish. Means the right soul. The one God chose for you. Your soulmate!"

They went into the moadon. Jenny put on the kettle to make coffee.

"Look, Jenny," Joe said, as he handed her the invitation, "Charlie… err…Hanoch gave me this. They're getting married in four weeks."

"Mazel Tov!"

"Kedumim? Hanoch, you, and Tamar are involved in Gush Emunim?" Jenny asked, staring at them, and reading the card again.

Jenny fell silent, contemplating the information. Her brow was wrinkled with concern. The few kibbutz members sitting in the moadon were staring at them; everyone was listening to their conversation. Joe was feeling very uncomfortable now.

"Yes, we want to prevent the government from giving up any land to the Arabs. The whole land was promised to us by Hashem…"

Wow. I read about this in the paper. They're nuts.

He saw the faces of the people looking at them as Tamar and Hanoch spoke.

"You were there illegally, weren't you? The army had to drag you away many times." He reminded them.

"Five times, to be exact." Tamar sounded proud saying that.

"So what! It's our country, not theirs!" Charlie-Hanoch had begun to raise his voice, seeing the looks he was getting.

"Yes, Baruch Hashem, we were allowed to stay in the army base there, near the Arab village of Kadum. Now there's another settlement, and there'll be more. Many more... a "geula shlema"!" Tamar lectured them with conviction.

"What does that mean?" Jenny asked.

"You know – a complete redemption! The in-gathering of all the exiles, the rebuilding of the temple – a third and final one!" Tamar continued.

"Oh, but isn't there a mosque or two there on the spot in Jerusalem? A hell of a lot of Arabs and millions of other Muslims mightn't appreciate the change," Joe commented.

"It's the time of the messianic age... all that will change. Soon. A little dynamite can go a long way!" Tamar was smiling, her eyes bright, as she spoke. "With God on our side..."

"Isn't there a Dylan song with a title like that ?" Joe joked, interrupting her, but neither of them responded to that.

Jenny understood and winked at Joe. He wondered if they'd heard him.

They sound crazed, totally out of touch with reality, Joe thought, but he couldn't resist asking a pointed question: "You know there are a lot of Arabs there in East Jerusalem and in the West Bank. What you call Judea and Samaria is full of them, maybe a couple of million. They think the land is theirs, that we're stealing it from them," Joe pointed out, now frustrated by the conversation.

The other kibbutz members had quietly left the room as they continued.

"I know, but they'll have to leave. They'll have to go back to Arabia where they're from, or accept our rule and keep their heads down. That's what Maimonides says..." Hanoch explained.

"That's not exactly democratic. And it's against international law, the Geneva Convention... isn't that so?" Joe was having trouble containing his anger now.

"You're talking goyische talk. We're not Europeans! When, Be'ezrat Hashem, all the Jews from the Diaspora come we'll be a majority in Eretz Israel, even in the areas of Judea and Samaria," Tamar answered.

"And who cares about international law, anyway. Umm Shmum! After what they did to the Jews of Europe why should we listen to them? Did they do anything to save our people when your family and mine were being slaughtered in places like Auschwitz, where they had nowhere to go, and no escape! No, they did nothing," Hanoch said, gripping the table as he shouted.

"Listen Hanoch, Tamar… it's getting late. Maybe you'd like to stay the night. You've a long way to drive back in the dark to get home to the Shomron. It's dangerous," Jenny said, her voice calm.

She's being sweet as always, despite our argument with them but I'd be happy if they left now.

"It's OK, Jenny, but thank you. We'll head home. You don't need to worry about us. And I have a weapon, see."

Hanoch lifted out an ugly black implement from its holster, waving it in front of them. Joe was taken aback by the pistol.

"You're coming to our wedding, right?"

Joe wondered whether that was an innocent question. It almost sounded like a threat! He completed the sentence in his mind… Or I will shoot you… but realized that was absurd.

"Eh... Yes… of course. Even if we don't agree politically… still friends, right?"

Everyone laughed, but the tension was still in the air.

Hanoch and Tamar left. Joe watched them get into their battered old car and drive off out to the pitch-black Golan Road. He felt a dark cloud of sadness, even fear, descending upon him.

"They're settlers, and so extreme…"

"We're settlers too."

"Yes, but not fanatics like them."

Days passed. Weeks passed. He waited to hear from Bora again.

CHAPTER 19

The army transferred Joe north to the Golan Heights, not far from the kibbutz. He rejoined his old unit. Nothing eventful happened. Guard duty followed guard duty. He got home often on leave.

Jenny stopped working in the moadon. After further training in first aid, she became a full-time nurse's aide, and applied to study nursing. She was accepted, but had to wait for the kibbutz to agree to let her go. There was a queue of members for studies outside. She was happy with the change, as she had tired of serving people coffee and tea, and cleaning up the moadon after them, but frustrated that she couldn't yet start studying.

Joe and Jenny started talking about starting a family.

Months passed. Joe was released from the army. He was asked to sign on as a non-commissioned officer, asked if he might be interested in an officer's course, having made a good name for himself as the platoon sergeant. He declined, despite the social pressure. He'd had enough of army service and was happy to go back to civilian life on the kibbutz. He came home, went back to gardening, enjoying mowing lawns with Maurice's little tractor again, and planting trees and shrubs to beautify their communal home.

Maurice had remarried. That and the fact that Joe was now an army veteran led to a friendlier relationship between them. He even invited Joe and Jenny around for afternoon coffee a couple of times.

Once a week on Tuesday evenings, Joe and Jenny would travel in the kibbutz van with three other kibbutz members to Ramat Magshimim to participate in Judaism classes. The teacher, Yedidya Cohen, had been a paratrooper in the same unit as some of the founders of Afikei Kinneret. One of his army friends posted the invitation to the class on the kibbutz notice board. Joe's conversations with Hanoch and Tamar aroused their interest in learning more about the religion. They enjoyed the classes. Yedidya had a sense of humour, and they were happy to meet new people from another world.

Yedidya had deep, profound eyes, a Herzl-like beard of

luxuriant dark curls and was erudite not only in Bible and Talmud but world literature as well. He loved to quote Tolstoy and Shakespeare as well as Rabbi Abraham Isaac Kook and A. D. Gordon, the Labour Zionist thinker. Unlike Hanoch and Tamar, he espoused moderate views regarding relations with the Arabs.

Chapter 20

BORA CALLS

Three months later Bora called.

They had just discovered that Jenny was pregnant, had returned from a visit to the gynaecologist in Tiberias that afternoon. It was early evening as the kibbutz van set out for home.

The burnt-out tractor was long gone, but the broken barbed wire fences and warnings of undiscovered Syrian mine fields were still there as always, as they drove back up the snake route to the kibbutz. Nachshon, no longer as cautious as he'd been after the accident, was speeding around the curves, Joe holding Jenny's hand and gripping the side of the van to steady them for safety's sake.

He wants to get back to the kibbutz before dark, but I wish he'd slow down.

"We're going to have a baby, Jenny, can you believe it? Are you as excited as I am?"

"Yes. But it's scary. I wasn't ready for this yet. I was hoping to go to nursing school first. It won't be just you and me any longer, Joe."

"I thought you wanted a baby!"

"I did, but not now. It's a lot of responsibility and we need to think about what it means for us, for our lives."

"Don't tell anyone. Not yet. It's early. Let's wait until we're sure everything's all right."

"OK, that makes sense, Joe."

They drove into the kibbutz; Nachshon parked the van and they went into the dining hall. Selma was there clearing away the last things after lunch. She was cheerfully singing to herself, her good-natured plump face turned towards the door to see who had entered the room.

"Anything left to eat, Selma?"

"I can put something together for you two lovebirds. Welcome home! Jenny, are you all right? You look pale. Here, sit down."

Selma disappeared into the kitchen, then returned with a tray piled with bread, salad, two plates with schnitzels and mashed potatoes. Beaming with pleasure at pampering them, she smiled kindly at them. She half asked, half declared: "You're pregnant aren't you, Jenny!"

They both laughed uncomfortably.

"Don't tell anyone yet!" Jenny scolded her.

"Of course, I won't!"

"Oh, in all the excitement I forgot to tell you, Joe. There was a phone call for you during lunch. It was hard to hear over the din here, but I wrote down the guy's name and phone number. He sounded old and had a Yiddish accent. He asked you to call him back."

"Now where did I put that note?"

She dug into her apron pocket, then into her jeans side pocket.

"Here it is," she said and handed it to Joe.

He read the scribbled name: "Joseph Borowski".

Joe phoned the number in the now empty dining hall. His hand shook as he reached for the phone. Each turn of the dial brought him closer to personal contact with the man who had been haunting him for years. He wasn't sure he wanted to meet him anymore, but he waited on the line, resisting the temptation to hang up, to flee. The telephone at the other end rang and rang. Finally, someone lifted up the receiver.

"Am I speaking to Joseph Borowski?" Joe could hear the nervous strain in his own voice as he asked.

"Who is this? Who wants to know?" It was a deep resonant voice; the Hebrew had a Yiddish intonation.

"This is Joe Kamens. Yanosh, and Eva's son. I'm returning your call…"

"Yes, Yossi, I know whose son you are. Are you on the kibbutz now?"

"Yes. I'm on the kibbutz."

Joe felt a surge of anger as he spoke to the old man.

Why did he contact me only now? What does he want from me? I don't like the way he talks to me, like an army officer giving orders.

"I'll be in the area tomorrow morning. If you are home, then I will come by. We can talk in person."

"Ah... Yes, I'll be home."

"Good. I will be there at 10:00 tomorrow morning. Where will you be?"

"I'll wait for you near the member's moadon. Just below the dining hall. Either there or out on the path near the parking lot, working in the garden."

"Yes. I know the place. Beautiful view there. Beautiful. See you in the morning."

The phone call ended, and he was gone again. Just the dial tone buzzing in Joe's ear remained at the other end of the line. He returned the receiver to its cradle, his hand still shaking.

It was a rough night. Joe slept poorly. Jenny went off to work early, leaving him with his thoughts and nervousness.

After breakfast he went to the tool shed determined to behave as he would on any workday. He prepared what he needed for the day's work, straining to focus on the task at hand. He took out a pair of cloth gardening gloves, a spray-can of weedkiller, a big plastic bucket, and a pair of pruning shears. Joe had the place to himself. Maurice was away at the Beit Berl Institute, but had instructed him the day before: "It's time for a manicure. While I'm away please tend to the paths in the centre of the kibbutz, around the office, the dining hall and the moadon."

He set out to follow those instructions rather than to continue to obsess about Bora's visit. He began trimming the rose bushes growing out over the paths and weeding the stone edges around them.

Every time a vehicle drove into the parking lot Joe looked up from his work to see if it might be Bora. The empty morning bus roared in, and the waiting two women boarded, carrying their empty shopping bags. The driver, with whom Joe was friendly, waved good morning as he passed him on his way out. A Tnuva delivery truck drove in, unloaded the day's dairy supplies, and left. So did the bakery delivery van. Nachshon drove up on his way out to Tiberias, and on to the Tel Aviv kibbutz offices. He had no passengers today.

"Waiting for someone?"

"What makes you say that?"

"I saw through the hadar ochel window how your head kept going up and down every time something drove in here."

"Well, yeah. I am expecting a visitor. An old friend of my family."

"Interesting. And he's coming all the way up here to the Golan? We don't often get visitors here."

Nachshon drove off.

The kibbutz van needs attention. Ought to be in the garage, before there's another accident, Joe thought to himself, noticing the dark smoke coming from the exhaust, trailing behind the old van as it moved out into the main road.

Joe's mind flashed back to that day, the images of the burnt vehicle, the helicopter, the bodies being carried away. He shuddered, then remembered where he was and why.

Where's Bora?

Joe looked at his watch. It was 10:15. No Bora.

He went back to work, trying to yank out the stubborn thick root of an unidentified weed. It reminded him of his struggle with his parents' past, with the mystery of this man Bora whom he was waiting to meet. He succeeded, almost falling backwards as it at last came out. As he wiped his sweaty brow with his sleeve, he heard a vehicle approaching. He strained his eyes to see a cloud of dust coming down the road, then recognized the dark form of an army jeep approaching. It turned into the kibbutz entrance and drove through past the guard box.

The jeep pulled up near him and a young red-haired officer hopped out from behind the wheel. Inside, he saw a bald head, two tufts of curly white hair on either side. The soldier opened the side door. A wooden walking stick emerged first, then a black, polished, leather shoe. A short stocky man stepped out. He looked familiar, but much older than in the pictures he knew from the past. He noticed that the left side of his face was scarred.

"Shalom Aleichem, Mr. Yossi!"

The same deep voice he'd heard on the phone. Bora. It's him.

"Hello... shalom, Mr. Borowski."

The man limped over to him and stretched out his hand. It, too, was scarred. Scars of this kind were familiar to him from his army days. Burn scars. Scorched skin.

The grip was strong, the dark brown eyes looking up into his were jocular and mischievous.

"Nice to meet you. And Mazal Tov on your recent marriage! I look forward to meeting your wife... Moshe, come back to pick me up in a couple of hours, all right. I will be down there in that far building – their moadon. Thank you. Come on, Yossi, let's go down there to talk."

He took Joe's arm and, limping, led him down the path past the dining hall to the moadon.

"My work doesn't allow me to be too specific about how I know things, certainly not on the telephone, Yossi, but I can tell you that I knew you were in the country from my friend Rivka. Later she also told me that you had settled here and volunteered for the army. You endangered your Australian citizenship by doing that, but we will take care of that problem."

"Rivka! But she didn't tell me anything about being in contact with you..."

"No, she couldn't. I told her not to. We were in contact after Gershon died, just before his funeral, but I don't want to talk further about that. We have other matters to discuss."

They entered the little concrete building. While Joe prepared coffee, Bora studied the decor in the room. A picture of young soldiers caught his eye.

"Nice club house you have up here. These soldiers here were members of the kibbutz killed in the Yom Kippur war?"

"Yes. Those two were. The third died in a training accident."

Bora looked more carefully at the photo, then looked up. Their eyes met for a moment, Joe saw that Bora's jocular look was gone now, replaced by deep sadness.

"We paid a heavy price in that war," Bora said, more to himself than to Joe.

He pointed to the shining blue-green lake below: "Are you happy here, Yossi?" he said, placing his hand on Joe's shoulder.

"Yes. I am. And I love that view! You've been here before?"

Joe moved away a little, reclaiming his personal space.

"I have. I know the landscape well."

"When was that?"

Bora sat down, beckoned to Joe to join him, and took a sip of coffee before replying as Joe sat down opposite him.

"When a group of soldiers, recently released paratroopers, wanted to come up here to create a kibbutz in 1968, they asked me to speak to people I knew in the government to get their support. I came up several times back then to see the place and discuss the idea with them. It had been a Syrian army base called Emrit Ez Edeen."

"But why did they ask you? What connection did you have to all of that?"

"Well, I have been a kibbutz member at Beit Alfa many years now. My sabra son Dani was born there. He was one of those paratroopers who had taken out the Syrian guns here, at a heavy price. Dani asked me to help them out; I made some phone calls and convinced friends in high places to support their plan."

"Dani, of the infamous tractor accident? I was there. I saw that. It happened the day I came up to the kibbutz. It was terrible. He was lucky to come out of it alive. The three others, the volunteers, weren't so lucky."

"Yes. That's right. I'm sure it was traumatic for you. It was a tragedy. For my son… it almost destroyed his life."

Joe softened at hearing this.

Oh my God, what a story! Poor man.

"I know. I heard he had a nervous breakdown… he never came back to the kibbutz again," Joe said.

Bora got up and walked over to the window, standing silently above the view, with his back to the room.

Joe joined him, placed his hand on Bora's shoulder in as gentle a manner as he could manage, but Bora moved away, sat down again.

This is heavy and has become some kind of strange dance between us, coming close then moving away, Joe thought.

Joe sat down as well.

Bora broke the silence: "He still hasn't fully recovered. A sensitive man, my son, despite the tough exterior and his many military exploits. He still struggles with guilt, but he has started a new life in Tel Aviv… But I didn't come up here to talk about Dani. I came to meet you."

Joe took his first sip of the now-cold sweet coffee.

"I'm sorry about all that. It's good to hear that your son has picked up the pieces and gone on with his life. It must've been very difficult for you."

"It was. I have been involved in many tough situations, as you know, but this was the hardest. But all that's in the past. There's something I want to talk to you about. I want to get down to brass tacks, to talk *tachles*."

"Wait a minute, Mr. Borowski. I've something I want to ask you first…"

"Call me Bora, as everyone does. What's on your mind?"

"My parents told me a lot about you, that you helped them escape the Communists…"

Bora's strange, mischievous smile had returned.

You were involved in some shady stuff, weren't you?"

That jocular gleam in his eyes was back.

"You could say that. I was settling accounts with Nazi murderers, S.S. men. Yanosh helped. Eva was nervous about it. She was expecting, and convinced Yanosh to stop."

"She told me she owed you for saving her and my father back then…"

"OK Yossi, but let's get to the point. What is it you want to ask?"

"What were you doing in Australia back then after the war?"

"You talked to Gershon, may he rest in peace, didn't you?"

"Yes, the day before he died."

"So, you know what you need to know. I got that S.S. mass murderer in the end. Justice was done."

"How do you know I spoke to Gershon?"

"I spoke to Gershon the night he died. He called me overseas to say goodbye. He told me he had spoken to you."

"Yes, I did. Gershon told me about the Avengers, which I realized later was like a confession, but he didn't help to contact you."

"He couldn't. I knew he was going to suicide, but you know he had cancer. He didn't have long, wanted to escape the pain, and not be a burden. We spoke about it before I left for Russia, and again in that last phone call."

"Russia?"

"Yes, helping smuggle Jewish activists out of there. I couldn't come. I was undercover at the time."

"Well. That is why I am here, Yossi. I didn't come to schmooze. I want your help."

"You want my help? Me?"

Bora nodded. Joe waited, but then a rowdy bunch of American tourists came into the building. Their guide, in shorts and sporting a moustache of gigantic proportions, silenced them, led them to the picture window to explain the view spread below and began telling the story of the conquest of the Golan in the Six-Day war.

Uggh, I hate these loud tourists and all their dumb questions!

Bora brusquely grabbed Joe's arm and pulled him out the door.

"Yes, I want to explain, but not here. We must move... somewhere more discreet... where we can talk without being overheard. And I would like to meet your kallah, your new wife, afterwards."

"Eh...we could walk down to the path down there." Joe said, pointing to the path. We can talk as we walk along the edge."

"No. That's too public."

"Then let's go back to my room. Jenny's still at work now… and I have something to give you…"

"Interesting."

Joe led Bora along the internal kibbutz path past the concrete blocks of the volunteers, soldiers, and single members, passed his old room. The olive sapling he'd planted was now a little tree. He pointed out the tree as they passed.

"I planted that tree. I used to live here before I got married."

"A truly Zionist act to plant a tree up here," Bora commented as they continued walking.

"Oh. So, you're not opposed to settlement across the green line like my father?"

"Listen, Joe, I make a distinction between settlement for security purposes and settlement because of crazy messianic ideas like your Gush Emunim friends."

Joe's mouth dropped.

"How do you know that?"

"We have our ways."

This is spooky. I'm being watched! I don't like this at all.

"And you don't care that it's against international law or about the UN condemnations?"

"No. Of course not. They are hypocrites. No, we must be tough, and smart, to survive here in the Middle East. As the Talmud teaches: 'Be like a reed: bend with the wind, but never break'. We can't let our enemies control a strategic place like this, can we? But we don't need to control an antagonistic population either to hold on to what we need for security."

"Makes sense to me."

Bora's approach sounded pragmatic and realistic. He thought of Hanoch and Tamar, their determination to settle in the middle of an Arab population that hated them. They wanted to hold onto the whole of the Land of Israel, whatever the cost. He rejected their ethnocentric morality. What kind of God did they believe in? Bora was no believer, but his devotion to Jewish survival was obvious and maybe more morally cogent.

They reached the neat row of family "cottages", each with its little garden out front. Some had plastic chairs and a table, or a cane rocking chair, there were others with artwork, metal sculptures by Matityahu, the resident "artist" who worked in the garage and gave gifts to his friends.

Unlike most of the other kibbutz homes, theirs had a mezuzah on the doorpost, as in any traditional Jewish home. It was a delicate blue colour. He'd bought it in Safed for their housewarming party the week before they were married and thought of it as a decorative good luck charm worth having in their new home, not as a religious obligation to be fulfilled.

Jenny and Joe had not yet fixed up their space much, but he'd planted a small lawn of rough grass and skirted it with a modest flower garden.

Europe has come to the Golan

He turned on the sprinkler before they walked into the building. "We need to irrigate this time of year up here," he explained.

"Making the desert bloom!"

Bora sounded ironic; his smile was strange.

"Well… it isn't exactly a desert here, but yes… I suppose you could say that. The Syrians didn't do much to develop this place before us."

Bora inspected the small living quarters with a knowing smile.

"How big is this unit?" he asked.

"About sixty metres. Two rooms. This kitchenette and living room and a small bedroom which is just space for a double bed, not much else."

"Books on nursing. Your wife is a nurse?"

"She wants to be. She's a nurse's aide in our little infirmary."

"And you?"

"I'm interested in agriculture, horticulture. My university degree was in biology."

"That I know. And you were a good student."

"Yes, I was, but now I'm enjoying working as a gardener here. It's soothing and quiet after my army service, but that's a temporary arrangement… until I figure out where I want to focus my energies."

"You didn't see much action, did you?"

"No. Not much. I suppose I was lucky that way, although I found that disappointing."

Bora laughed at hearing that.

Joe was starting to get irritated with this strange man and what felt like a cross examination.

"There's plenty of reserve duty to come. You never know what the future holds. You might still be honoured with some excitement."

Bora's eyes and mouth formed a bizarre smile as he said this.

"Umm... I know... but... anyway what was it you wanted to talk to me about?"

"Yes. Tachles, down to brass tacks!"

Joe laughed nervously.

"I want you to come down to Tel Aviv to meet someone there. I have a proposal for you, one you might find very interesting. A small job for you to do. You will need preparation, some training."

"I don't understand what you're talking about. Can you be more specific, more explicit?"

"No. Not at this stage, but I do want to know if you are willing to travel overseas, using your Australian passport. Are you willing to help us? To help Jews overseas in trouble?"

"Maybe... maybe. I'll have to think about it. You know Jenny is pregnant..."

"Yes, I do. Mazal tov. I've faced that issue in the past with your family, as you know."

Another strange laugh from him and then:

"Nu? And?"

"She's expecting and I just got out of the army. It's not so simple to just go off overseas. In any case, I would need permission from the kibbutz."

"That can be arranged. Think about it."

"I will. You know I just remembered that we do have something alcoholic to drink if you would like. I have a small bottle of vodka someone left us."

"Perfect, but let's wait until your wife gets here and then we'll drink leHaim together. And didn't you say there was something you wanted to give me?"

"Yes. I'll get it... Just a moment."

Joe went into the bedroom and pulled the old coat down from the overhead "boydem" storage space. He dusted it off.

"Here, Bora, this was once yours."

Joe felt a strange sadness as he handed the old man his beloved coat. Bora held up the coat to look at it, then returned it to Joe.

"Ah, yes. It's a telogreika, the kind of coat we wore in the forest during the war."

"It's yours. My parents had it. I brought it here all the way from Melbourne for you."

"You can keep the coat. I don't need it. I see you are attached to it, but for me it only brings back bad memories."

Bora was frowning as he spoke. His eyes were icy.

Joe's heart fell at hearing this.

After all my effort to bring the coat, to take good care of it, and despite my willingness to sacrifice it to its original owner... This?

He felt disappointed, let down.

But... maybe... I should have realized... Bora wanted to get rid of the coat! That's why he left it behind in Australia. Instead of doing something good for the man I've done the opposite, brought him a reminder of a past he wanted to forget! How could I have been so stupid?

"Um... but I thought you'd be happy to have it back," Joe mumbled.

"No. Not at all."

"I hear someone coming now..."

Jenny came home tired and upset. Joe could tell when she walked through the door that something had happened at work. He noticed blood stains on her tunic. He knew that look on her face. There was a fleeting expression of "Oh, no!" when she first saw Bora sitting there, his bald head shining in the afternoon sun as she came in through the entrance door. He saw how she put a smile on her face for the guest.

"Hi, darling! This is Joseph Borowski. You know, the famous Bora."

"Hello, Mr. Borowski. Nice to meet you."

"Shalom, Mrs. Kamens. Just call me Bora, like your husband does. I am honoured to meet Joe's bride."

Bora bowed his head a little in Jenny's direction.

"Thank you...eh...you'll have to excuse me for a moment."

Jenny said. She headed for the bedroom. "I'll just get out of my work clothes. I'm sure Joe is taking good care of you."

"He is, he is… and he offered to give me this old coat of his."

"But Bora refused to take it back. Here, darling, maybe you can toss it on the bed on your way."

"That coat again! You should get rid of it."

Jenny left the room, leaving the coat behind.

"Excuse me, Bora."

Joe got up, took the coat, and followed her into the bedroom. He threw the coat up into the boydem, then turned to her: "What's going on Jen?"

"What do you mean?"

"I saw the look on your face when you came in. And look at that blood-stained tunic of yours. What happened? What's the matter?"

"It was a bad day at work. One of the kids, Reuven, you know Itamar and Yael's son…"

"What happened?"

"He cut his fingers fooling around with a sharp banana knife, almost severed two of them. There was a lot of blood, and hysterical parents to deal with… the ambulance was slow in coming back from outside the kibbutz to take him. I'm not sure they'll be able to save that hand. Sarah went off with the ambulance and left me to deal with the rest, and I had a lot of fluey, sick kids and kindergarten teachers to deal with through the day."

"I guess it isn't a good day to have a guest after work."

"No. But I'll do my best."

Joe blew her a kiss.

"I know Bora is important to you. Maybe after we water him you could take him for a walk or something?"

"I've been with him for a while now. He just wanted to meet you before leaving."

Joe decided that it was not a good time to mention Bora's request. That would have to wait.

"OK. I'll be out in a minute. Meanwhile, I need to soak this tunic right away in a basin of cold water."

Joe emerged to find Bora flipping through a magazine.

"Is everything all right, Yossi?"

"She just had a rough day in the infirmary. She'll join us soon."

Jenny emerged from the bedroom wearing white shorts and a short-sleeved green blouse that highlighted her green eyes. She had untied her long auburn hair whose rich colour looked reddish in the afternoon sun. She looked more relaxed now.

Joe went back into the kitchenette while Bora and Jenny exchanged a few words. He returned with a bottle of beer, a pitcher of water and three glasses.

"Sorry, couldn't find the vodka I promised. We'll have some beer."

Bora held out his glass which Joe filled; Jenny poured herself a glass of water.

Bora raised his glass, and offered a toast:

"To the young couple and their future progeny. LeHaim!"

"LeHaim!"

Jenny sipped her water, finally managing a smile. Bora finished his beer, rose to leave, and handed Joe a business card.

"Call me soon," he said, and left.

Joe looked down at the card.

"Colonel Joseph Borowski, Special Projects, Ministry of Defence," it read.

"He's a charming man, your friend, Bora." Jenny sounded sarcastic.

Jenny picked up and read the business card: "Joe, I think he's a good person to know. You know, vitamin P – protectzia."

Chapter 21

Bora's Invitation

A letter came from Tel Aviv for Joe Kamens. No markings or return address appeared on the envelope. He opened it:

Dear Joe,

I look forward to seeing you again. I have a proposition for you, as I told you when I visited a couple of weeks ago, it is an opportunity to serve your country and to help fellow Jews in need. The rest I will tell you in person. Please contact me at this number 03-57648 any evening and we will arrange a meeting here in Tel Aviv. There are some people here that I work with who would like to meet you.

Kol Tuv,

Joseph Borowski

The handwriting was neat and tight, but each sentence ended with a final, long stroked, letter, in flight across the page, a flourish of ink.

Joe obsessed about this repeated request.

Should I respond? Should I ignore it? Should I contact Bora despite my misgivings? I'll discuss it with Jenny and then come to a decision.

He headed for the infirmary to look for her, but she wasn't there. He found her in the kibbutz dining room talking to Selma. They were both leaning forward in intense discussion about babies.

"Shalom Joe! Jenny told me you heard the heartbeat yesterday. You must be excited."

"Yes. I am ... it was incredible." Jenny broke into a broad smile at hearing this, but he wasn't smiling.

"Hi, Joe! What's the matter? You look worried about something."

"Uh. Yes. Let's talk about it later when you get home."

■■■

That evening when Jenny got home, they talked about Bora's invitation:

"Jen, darling, I'm not sure what do with this…"

"He invited you. You should go visit. We could take the day off to go to Tel Aviv. We can go to the beach. You know how much I love the sea. We haven't done that in a long time."

"Maybe. We could go to Tel Aviv, I suppose. He could be our excuse for a little holiday. To tell the truth, now that I've spoken to him, I'm not sure I want too much contact with him. He killed people… Nazis… after the war. Who knows what he does now… he kind of… eh… spooks me."

"Me too. I thought you looked nervous when he was here. Even so, he's a good contact to have, he helped your parents, helped this kibbutz get off the ground, might one day help us somehow, but be careful what you say to him and don't make any commitment."

"I don't know… What do I need contacts in the city for? I'm just a kibbutz gardener after all. By the way, how's little Reuven doing? You've been spending a lot of time on him."

"Yes, I have, and I'm happy I did. The doctors were able to save Reuven's hand. He needed a lot of stitches, and will need extensive physiotherapy, but has progressed well."

Jenny took it upon herself to follow up the case, to make sure the boy was doing the exercises the physiotherapist prescribed. The parents were very appreciative. They supported her request to the kibbutz to be allowed to go out to the nursing school in Haifa.

She was starting to show now, her cheeks were rosy, and she was glowing with health, more energetic than ever. Her pregnancy was no longer a secret.

But Joe wondered how his wife would manage to study through her first years as a new mother. Jenny assured him she could do it, with his help. Sarah, the nurse, was very supportive.

Jenny's belly continued growing, parenthood was fast approaching.

Chapter 22

TO TEL AVIV

Nachshon drove Joe down to Tiberias. There was no one driving to Tel Aviv that cold winter day, so he took the bus. He wore his partisan coat, tightly wrapped around him for protection against the cold wind and watched his steamy breath as he waited. Jenny decided not to come. She felt that in her condition, it would be too strenuous, and that in any case it was better for Joe to go alone. He agreed. Anyway, it was too cold to go to the beach this time of year.

The bus pulled up to the platform. People started boarding, pushing, and shoving to get in out of the cold. Joe boarded gratefully. He warmed himself by rubbing his hands together as they drove out of the city.

It was a slow bus that stopped in many places on the way. Afula was a longish stop. Joe grabbed a take-away coffee and a sandwich there. Being Sunday morning, the vehicle was full of soldiers, standing room only. There were also some Arab workers, and a couple of older women with brightly coloured plastic shopping baskets.

Outside it was grey, bleak, and darkening. Joe heard distant thunder coming closer and saw a flash of lightning across the horizon. It began to pour; heavy rain pounded on the roof of the bus, and then hailstones. The driver pulled over to wait until the main downpour ended. People in the bus started talking about the weather, expressed impatience. The driver ignored their comments, increased the volume of the radio. Arik Einstein singing "*Ani Veata nishaneh et haOlam* – You and I will change the world" drowned out the passengers' conversation and complaints. He restarted the engine. People cheered as the bus pulled away from the Afula curb, splashing passers-by as it increased speed.

The rain stopped. Joe could see out the bus window again. They drove out of town and through the Jezreel Valley. He saw its familiar patchwork of green and brown fields.

What a beautiful country.

He fell asleep, leaning on the window. Beside him sat a tall soldier who was all legs which left him little space. The only escape was sleep. He awoke as they drove into Tel Aviv. Soon they were pulling into the central bus station.

The lanky soldier next to him uncurled himself and got up out of the seat. Joe was finally freed from his cramped corner to get off the bus. Now he would go see what it was Bora wanted of him. He stretched and went down the aisle into the noisy market-place-like bus station. He had to get to an address on Hayarkon Street. He remembered the street as near the beach, a place of sleazy little hotels and street prostitution.

From the bus station he took the number 5 Dan bus to Dizengoff Street. As he was early for the meeting, he got off a stop earlier and walked down to the beach. That was the one thing he loved about Tel Aviv – the proximity of the sand and sea. It reminded him a little of Melbourne, where as a boy he'd often spent time at St. Kilda or Elwood beach. Although it was chilly, when he did reach the beach, he took off his shoes and walked along on the cold sand for a while, breathing in the salty sea air and trying to relax before the meeting. The familiar feel of the sand was calming.

He thought about what he had observed from the bus, on the way to the beach, and what he saw around him now while walking barefoot in the sand.

Tel Aviv had changed. Joe remembered walking along Dizengoff when he had first come to the country, past small shops, and restaurants. His mother had described it as a very special place. People were sitting in coffee shops, drinking, smoking, and talking as she had excitedly described, but the people he saw looked old, worn, and unhappy. It did feel Mediterranean, very different from the elegant Collins Street restaurant area back home, but it was not the exotic place he had expected. There were a couple of new hotels recently built, and, of course, the famous Shalom Tower, but most of what he saw looked old, run-down. It was not the romantic city of young

Hebrew writers and artists he had read about either.

He felt the cold and put his shoes back on. He wrapped himself more snuggly in his coat to protect himself from the strong wind that had begun to blow. He now appreciated that Bora had let him keep it.

It began drizzling.

Joe turned off the boardwalk back onto Hayarkon Street.

The address Bora had sent him was 5 Hayarkon Court, off Hayarkon Street, near the intersection with Gordon, not far from the Indian embassy. He couldn't find the place so after walking up and down twice he went into a camera store to ask for directions.

The unshaven storekeeper was gruff, but helpful. His shop was untidy, parts of cameras on the counter. The man pulled out a notepad and a pencil and drew him a quick map. His big ears twitched as he did so.

"Thank you, sir." Joe smiled at him.

The man softened.

"Strange address you're going to," he commented.

"What do you mean?"

"I walk past there twice a day. It's unmarked, no sign or number on the door and the people there are very secretive. It's set back next to the parking lot in that little lane."

"Sounds straightforward enough. I'm sure I'll find it now."

"A couple of guys from there came in here the other day looking to buy cameras that could be easily hidden. I told them I don't stock such things. They walked off without another word."

"How did you know they're from there?"

"I don't know for sure. Just a hunch. They came from that direction, didn't say much. It was a strange request."

"Anyway, thank you again. I've got to go."

"Be careful."

Joe found the place – a long, narrow, low prefabricated white building. He saw no sign or other markings anywhere but there was a red buzzer. He pressed it, heard a low brerrrrrr sound but nothing happened. He pressed it again.

The door opened. A tall, bearded man in a blue suit and glasses was standing opposite him, his face sphinx-like.

"Follow me," the man ordered. He started walking, Joe followed.

"Where am I?" Joe asked.

"You will soon see. Sit here. We will call you soon." The man's face was still expressionless.

Joe looked around him. He was in a small sitting room with a brown settee and a low wooden coffee table. He took off his coat, hung it on a peg, and then sat down. The couch was uncomfortable, hard. The walls were white and bare. He noticed an apparatus, a flat metallic object in the ceiling opposite him. Perhaps it's a smoke detector, maybe a hidden camera… hard to tell.

Joe sat there wondering what awaited him. He'd expected to meet Bora here, had expected an elegant office, not this. But so far, no trace of Bora.

He took his newspaper out of his bag, began unfolding it to continue working on the crossword puzzle on the back page. Unfolding his Jerusalem Post, a small headline on an inside page caught his eye. He hadn't noticed it before.

Mossad Agent Borowski to Be Honoured for Service to the People.

He looked at the photo below. It was Bora! The date was that day's date, Sunday, 8th February, 1976. He read the article, forgetting where he was:

Mossad Agent Borowski to Be Honoured for Service to the People

President Ephraim Katsir and Mossad director, Yitzhak Hofi gave Joseph Borowski, better known as Bora, a lifetime achievement commendation at a ceremony at the President's residence yesterday.

Bora's long career included clandestine operations that facilitated the immigration of tens of thousands of Jews to Israel from behind the iron curtain and from Arab lands.

Recently retired at the age of 64, he remains a senior advisor to the organization where his experience and knowledge are invaluable.

Health issues as well as his son Daniel's tragic suicide led to his decision to withdraw from active duty. Notable in the small audience in attendance was Issar Harel, commander of the unit that had captured Eichmann, and the well-known partisan poet Abba Kovner."

"Mister Kamens, please come with me."

Joe looked up from his newspaper still shocked about Dani's death to see a petite young woman in a business suit standing over him. Her blue eyes were blank, emotionless despite a slight smile on her lips. She repeated her request.

He got up to follow her, his eyes noting her swinging hips as they walked.

She led him through a metal door after walking along a dark corridor. They emerged into a brightly lit room. She closed the door behind without another word and was gone, leaving Joe standing there alone. He noticed a camera lens in the ceiling pointed towards him.

Two men entered the room; one greeted him briefly:

"Shalom, Kamens, take a seat."

The other pointed to the long wooden table in the centre of the room, at which there were three chairs.

There was no window, nor any decoration of any kind on the grey walls. He felt as if he had entered an inquisition chamber and wondered when they would produce their torture implements. They were both in dark business suits, were clean-shaven, had short-cropped hair and wore dark glasses. He laughed to himself nervously. *Why are they wearing sunglasses inside?*

"No need to be nervous, Yossi. Please sit down," the taller of the two said.

He sat down.

They also sat, opposite him.

"You were reading this morning's paper while you waited?"

"Yes."

"And you are from Australia originally."

"Yes, I am."

"Let's get down to business. You came because Bora sent you. He recommended you to us."

"Uh… Yes, that's true. Recommended me? Recommended for what?"

"The first question is whether you would be willing to serve your country? We see you have served in the I.D.F., that you live on a border kibbutz. All of that is commendable, but Israel needs more from you."

"You are asking me to join the Mossad?"

"No, not exactly, but there are particular needs that you can help with."

"Yes, but I don't… don't understand what you are talking about. Can you be more explicit please?"

The other silent guy spoke for the first time.

"You would be trained, of course. That is my department."

"Trained to do what? Why me?"

The taller one spoke again: "There are reasons, but we'll be more specific after you answer our initial question."

"Which question is that?"

"Whether you are interested in being of service again? Will you help us?"

"Not without knowing what this is all about. I don't like all this mystery, and I won't blindly commit to anything until I hear more details."

"Very well. Here is my card. If you change your mind, call me."

"That's it?"

"That's it."

They escorted Joe back to the waiting room without any further exchange of words. The petite woman in the business suit reappeared and led him, after he put on his partisan coat, to the front door.

"That's an interesting coat you have on."

"Yes. It is unusual, isn't it? It has travelled much of the world."

"It looks pretty old, and very warm."

"It is."

She winked at him, turned, and walked away. He watched her tight swinging hips disappear down the corridor, noticed her red shoes.

Out in the street again he was blinded by the Mediterranean sun, smelled the salt of the sea. He watched as a young couple passed by, walking arm in arm towards the beach carrying what looked like a picnic basket. An old one-armed man wearing a kaffiya was wheeled past in a wheelchair by a teenage boy.

Joe turned to walk back the way he had come, turned onto Hayarkon Street. He walked past the jewellery store, the camera store, and on towards his bus stop. He headed home, baffled, wondering what that was all about.

Why me? he asked himself.

That evening after work Jenny asked Joe about the trip to Tel Aviv. He was reluctant to talk about it.

"It was very strange, Jen. The whole thing gives me the creeps."

"So, you just ran away?"

"Yep. Listen, you're about to have a baby. It's not a time for me to get involved in the kind of stuff Bora does."

"Are you sure about that Joe? You've complained to me about our life here on the kibbutz, that it's kind of boring for you now. Every day the same… all of that."

"Maybe… but Bora's espionage stuff… that's not the change we need."

The next day Bora called the kibbutz. Selma waved Joe into the dining room and handed him the phone.

"Hello, Yossi."

"Hello. Bora?"

"Yes, it is I. What happened yesterday?"

"Nothing. I don't know what you people want from me, but I've decided I'm not interested."

"That's not the impression you gave me when I visited the kibbutz."

"I don't know why you thought I was interested in this stuff."

"Well, you did come down to Tel Aviv, didn't you?"

"Bora, please leave me alone!"

"Listen Yossi. I hear that you are upset. Let's talk about this again when you are calmer and have thought about our request, all right?"

Joe knew he was being rude to a national hero, the man he had so admired until recently. He felt manipulated by him, felt like a fly caught in a spider's web, Bora, the smiling spider waiting for him as his prey. The first surge of anger had subsided, but he still struggled to keep his anger to himself.

There was a long pause, Bora's patient breathing clearly audible through the phone receiver at his ear, and then he said:

"All right, Mr. Borowski, I'll call you back in a few days, but I don't think you'll hear a different answer then either. I'm sorry if I got hot under the collar just now. And congratulations on your recent award from the president."

"Thank you, Yossi. Have a good day. Give Jenny my regards."

"OK, Bye."

Joe wasn't sure about that.

Chapter 23

NEW LIFE

On the way to the hospital, between contractions, Jenny turned to Joe and said jokingly: "You know, Joe, you would have made a good spy."

He laughed.

"We have a more important project to focus on now!"

The next contraction ended that conversation.

The baby, a big and healthy girl, was born in the Poriah Hospital. She weighed three and a half kilos. They named her Rina.

Bora called a few times at first. Joe was polite but distant. Jenny would suggest they go visit the man sometime, but they never did.

Jenny and Joe didn't forget about Bora and the Mossad, but they set the whole thing aside, made a joke of it, overwhelmed as they were by their new responsibilities as parents. It came up in conversation sometimes. Joe wondered what life would have been like had he responded positively; he was flattered to have been asked, but that was all. Bora faded into the background of Joe's life after a time. Perhaps it had been wise to keep his distance.

Life flowed on without Bora. The coat was stored away and forgotten.

18th May 1977: "Did you hear the election results?" Joe called to Jenny in the shower cubicle one morning before work.

"No, why?"

"Labour lost! Menahem Begin is forming a government without them, a coalition with the religious parties."

He heard the water stream suddenly stop. Jenny's head poked out from behind the shower curtain, her hair dripping.

"What!?"

"Yes. I know... it's hard to believe."

Jenny stood there, now wrapped in a towel, disbelief written all over her face.

"You are joking, Joe!"

"No, I'm not. I've just heard the news on the radio. It's true."

"Begin? That demagogue? That's impossible. That's like the world coming to an end. What will that mean for the kibbutz movement, for us?"

"Now, you're being hysterical, Jen. Not like you."

He hugged her.

"The world didn't come to an end just because Begin became Prime Minister last night. Got to go to work," he said.

"Have a good day, darling. I guess it'll be all right."

The world didn't come to an end, but it changed. Sadat came to visit Israel. They watched his arrival on television, amazed. "No more war!" he said from the Knesset podium.

A peace agreement with Egypt followed. The country was overjoyed. Peace with the Arabs no longer seemed an impossible dream.

"It's like the messiah came," Selma commented at the weekly kibbutz meeting, "but we have to talk about new irrigation pipes now, not politics."

Everyone agreed. The kibbutz settled back into its normal life rhythm...

One Sunday morning after breakfast in the kibbutz dining hall, Joe remembered he hadn't collected his mail since Thursday. He finished his coffee, carried his tray over to the dish-washing machine and went to his letterbox to see what it contained.

Inside he found two letters and a postcard. The postcard was from Adam; on one side was a picture of a blue-green lake, labelled "near Dublin" and on the other a few scribbled words. He looked at the two letters: one was an aerogramme from his mother, the other an envelope from Judy.

I haven't heard from Judy in years, wonder what's up?

He folded the two letters and stuffed them and the postcard into the deep inside pocket of his old coat.

It was pouring outside now. He hummed Dylan's song "Shelter from the Storm" to himself as he stood at the door looking outside, waiting for it to subside, but it didn't.

He pulled up his hood, curled himself into the warm fur and walked out into the rain and wind. On the way to the car, he popped into their apartment to leave the mail there.

What does Judy want from me? Why has she suddenly written after a silence of years?

These thoughts accompanied him out to his car but were soon forgotten during a busy day.

That evening when he got home, wet, and tired, he remembered the letters. He opened his mother's first. A picture fell out onto the floor. He picked it up and looked at it, a photo of his parents and sister Lily. They were in bathing suits and were suntanned and smiling. Lily looked happier than she had before her divorce. He read:

Dear Joe,

We miss you very much. It's summer vacation here. The enclosed picture is from up north – Surfer's Paradise – where we've spent the past week. How are you? How's Jenny? My darling granddaughter, Rina? Did she like the doll I sent? We'll send more soon. Please send us more pictures and an update. We haven't heard from you in a while now. Write soon!

Love, Mum xxx

p.s. a friend of ours has brought a gift for you to Israel. He left it with Rivka on kibbutz Lochamei HaGetaot. She has been trying to contact you to come get it.

Joe handed the photo and page to Jenny to read too.

"Your mother is sweet, dear."

"Uh huh."

"It's time we visited Australia again."

"Maybe. But it's very expensive, and very far away. The end of the earth, really."

"They would help out."

"I'm sure they would. We'll talk about it. Right now, I have another letter from Australia I want to read."

"Who's it from?"

"An old friend of mine. Someone I haven't heard from in a long time."

"It's a woman, isn't it?"

"How do you know?"

"I looked at the envelope when I came in."

"Oh."

He ripped open the envelope. It gave off a scent, a familiar smell of scented oil; patchouli. He remembered that Judy had shown him that oil last time he saw her in Melbourne. The page was adorned with sketches of trees, flowers and impish-looking human faces. Judy loved drawing and had often been doodling or sketching when they were kids.

He began to read:

Melbourne, 23rd of February. 1979

Dear Joey,

Hi! How are you?

I bet you are surprised to hear from me! It has been a long, long time. Years. Maybe you've heard from your sister or from Adam when he was over there in Israel, about my marriage to Avi and my divorce and all that. Anyway, I want to belatedly say Mazel Tov! I heard from Lily that you got married to a girl you met on the kibbutz up there in the Golan. She told me her name is Jenny and showed me her picture, a photo of the two of you at the beach. You looked great. So relaxed! And she is pretty. And now you have a baby too! Wonderful. Please send me a photo of your little girl. So… not to keep you in suspense any longer, I'll get to the point. I'm coming for a visit this coming April. I have cousins in Ramat Gan, and they've invited me to the Seder this coming Pesach. I just finished my MA, and the timing is perfect for me so I booked a flight and will be spending three weeks in Israel.

Look forward to seeing you soon, Joey!

Xxxooo

Judy.

Ukhh! I hate being called that name, but that's what I was to Judy back then. I'm not that person anymore. She'll have to get used to calling me Joe like everyone else. And, anyway, yes, I've heard about her and Avi, about their messy divorce, the quarrel over money. Not my problem...

His sister, long a senior social worker in Melbourne, supported Judy through her rough time. Lily's divorce from Aubrey had been easier. No one was surprised they split up. She'd written about Judy's travails, but Joe wasn't interested. He'd tried to forget his old flame. The idea that Judy would be coming in a few months aroused old, buried emotions.

What does she want now after all these years? My life's getting tangled up like a ball of string full of knots. Jenny wanting to leave the kibbutz is one, Bora's lurking calls another, and now Judy! It's too much.

And Judy knew about Bora too. She knew about my obsession with the man, the part he'd played in my aliya decision. She laughed at me, told me I was crazy, that I should let it go, to leave the past alone. Imagine what kind of negative comments she would make about the Mossad connection. A killer, an assassin, that's your hero? I'd rather not see her again. I don't want to be told "I told you so!"

Jenny was staring at him. "What's the matter, Joe?"

"Nothing."

"You're upset about something. What did your old girlfriend write?"

"It's nothing, Jen. She's coming for a visit, that's all. And she was never a girlfriend!"

He tried to change the subject, to talk about the day's news, her work, his work, but she wouldn't let go. He smelled jealousy in her questions about the past, about his adolescent friendship with Judy.

"Look, Jenny. You're feeling jealous but you don't need to. Judy is nothing to me. I never slept with her. Just leave it alone, OK."

"All right Joe. Didn't mean to upset you. I think you are being very touchy."

He put the radio on, turned the dial to find some music on the army radio station, the Naomi Shemer song, "Lu Yehi". They sat listening, relaxed. They both loved the song.

Joe got up and brought them two cups of hot tea. The "Kaveret" group was singing nonsense "Poogie" songs now. Jenny looked him in the eyes, took his hand. She kissed him.

"I love you, Joe."

"I love you, too, Jenny."

They drank their tea in silence, listening to the music, laughing at the silly lyrics. Then, the broadcaster interrupted the music with a news flash. The voice on the radio was deep and calm but what he said was unnerving, and disturbing.

"There has been a terrorist attack in the north. At least one person killed. The terrorists are still at large. We will update you as soon as we know more."

"They never give up, those Arabs! They really hate us, want to kill us all."

"That's not true, Jenny. They aren't all the same. But these guys who infiltrated to kill Jews, they were trained... professional terrorists, I would guess. Really dangerous... and still out there on the loose!"

"It scares me. Makes me think it's better to stay here on this isolated kibbutz, and not move to the centre of the country after all. Maybe we are safer here."

"Jenny don't fool yourself. This kibbutz was the site of terrible battles. There is nowhere in this country that is free of our bloody struggle with the Arabs over this tiny piece of earth."

"Will it never stop? After everything the Jews have gone through, like what happened to your parents and their families in Poland... isn't it enough already!"

They sat there in silence as the radio sounded the dirge-like patriotic music it always did when something like this happened. Joe thought of their family's future in Israel, that his kids too would have to go to the army, but he kept that to himself. He wondered what Jenny was thinking about and glanced at her, concerned at her worried look. He could see how tired his wife was and wasn't surprised at what she next said:

"I'm going to bed, Joe. We'll know what happened in the morning."

"Go ahead. I'm staying up a little longer. Sleep well."

"Maybe we should think of leaving the country altogether…"

"Don't be silly…"

Jenny withdrew into their bedroom, then re-emerged in her nightgown.

"Goodnight, darling."

"I'll be there soon."

He sat there staring out the window at nothing. It was less windy now but still raining steadily.

It will be muddy tomorrow.

Beyond the silhouette of the bush outside their window he could see, through the steady rainfall, the shimmering reflection of light coming from their neighbour's apartment. That light went out, and darkness ruled outside. He listened to the gentle sound of the falling rain. After a while his eyes started to close.

Maybe I should hit the sack?

He got up and headed for the toilet, starting the nightly ritual before going to bed. He glanced in to see Jenny lying in bed asleep, her book opened on her chest. The book rose and fell slightly with each breath.

She looks peaceful; I won't disturb her by turning off her light yet.

He knew that if he did so, she would awake and protest that she was still reading.

He returned to the sofa and switched the radio on, lowering the volume. They were still playing sad music. He heard the announcer's voice, no longer calm, saying something. What is he saying? He listened more carefully, turned the volume up again.

"Four Palestinian terrorists landed on Nahariya beach late this evening in a motorized rubber boat. Heavily armed, the four entered a shorefront housing complex, knocked on the door, spoke into the

intercom in Arabic, then moved on to knock on another. Terrified residents informed the police. One of the citizens was armed with a pistol and shot one of the terrorists dead. They shot and killed one police officer. They then shot down the door of one of the nearby homes. They have taken two hostages, a man, and his daughter. The building is surrounded. The police are negotiating with the three terrorists, one of whom speaks some Hebrew."

"Oh, my God! This is bad."

"Jenny was standing there, rubbing her eyes.

"What happened?"

"The… the Arab terrorists… they've killed a policeman, and now they've taken hostages."

"What's going to happen? What do they want?"

"Release of Palestinian prisoners. The army is playing for time before they go in. They will try to calm the situation, while they prepare to send in a special commando unit to break in, take them by surprise, and free the hostages, the man, and his daughter."

"Doesn't sound good…"

"No, it's a huge dilemma. Not much chance of success. Not likely that anyone in that apartment will come out of this alive. If they don't break in, those animals will almost certainly kill them…"

"Joe, we've got to go to work in the morning. That's soon. It's already two thirty-five now. You're disturbing me listening to the radio here."

"Oh, I'm sorry. I guess it is very late."

"You can't help anyone by listening all night. Turn it off. Come to bed."

He nodded and joined her in bed. They lay awake, each thinking, tense. Jenny turned to him, caressed his shoulders and neck.

"Relax, Joe, relax."

It felt good.

His eyes slowly closed. He dreamed that night that he was

there in Nahariya, that he was one of those soldiers waiting to storm that apartment to free the hostages. Then he heard Jenny suddenly cry out in her sleep. That woke him. He looked over at her. She was curled up under the blankets, facing the other way, still fast asleep. He turned the other way, tried to relax, and go back to his dream, to see what would happen next.

It was hopeless; he was wide awake now. He bent over to kiss her gently, got up, looked out to see the stars beyond the tree he'd planted, *Will there ever be peace here?* he wondered, as he became drowsy, then fell asleep.

Morning sunbeams woke him. He looked up at the kitchen clock to see the time was 6:00 a.m. He'd spent the night asleep on the chair by the window.

When the alarm rang, Jenny was already in the shower. He put on the kettle and asked her when she would be out.

"I need to get going, it's late!" he yelled through the bathroom door.

She came out wrapped in a towel, glowing. "It's all yours."

Jenny was listening to the news on the radio. Joe showered, dressed, and joined her at the half table in the kitchenette. Two cups of coffee were steaming there. She was crying, her cheeks wet.

"What happened last night in Nahariya?" Joe asked.

"It's horrible. The terrorists shot their way out, using the man, and his four-year-old daughter as cover, and made a run for the beach. There was shooting out there. Two of the terrorists were captured, one killed. But before all that... when they found their rubber dinghy full of bullet holes they murdered the man in front of his daughter, shot him in the back. They murdered the child too. They smashed her skull against the rocks there before the police and army got there."

He sat down beside her, took her hand, sighed.

"There's more..."

"That's not all?"

"No, there is worse. The woman, the mother, survived, but her baby didn't."

"What do you mean?"

"In the mayhem, during the shooting, she hid under a bed where they couldn't see her…"

"Smart lady…"

"And when the baby started to make a sound, she covered her mouth and smothered her to death."

"Oh, my God!"

"It's unbelievable. Just like the stories we've heard from Poland during the Holocaust. How can a mother live with that? I wouldn't be able to." She started crying again.

"It is terrible, terrible… but Jenny, calm down. We have to go to work… get on with our normal routine…"

The radio announcer was saying something more; Joe turned up the radio volume to hear better:

"The murdered hostages have been identified as Danny and Einat Haran. The baby that died in the family home was Yael Haran. Two policemen were killed."

Then, he added more details. Joe and Jenny, their coffee untouched, listened to the words:

"The terrorists are from a Palestinian refugee camp in Lebanon. They belong to the PLF, the Palestine Liberation Front. The group leader, Samir Kuntur, was taken alive. He was 16 years old."

"16 years old? Just a kid!" Jenny exclaimed.

Just a kid, but already a murderer. Shocking… He must have been educated to hate. Where are we living? What kind of future is there here?

"I wish they would have killed him too," Joe said and left for work, without having touched his coffee. Jenny was still sitting there, staring at the radio, drying her eyes and sipping her now-cold coffee.

■■■

Judy never came. She cancelled her flight because of her ill mother, who died a month later of lung cancer. Lily informed Joe about what had happened, explained that Judy was very depressed, and she was trying to help her, that a letter from him would help. He sent his condolences. She never replied.

He wondered about the kind of relationship they might have had, had he stayed in Australia. He would never know.

Joe and Jenny stayed on at Kibbutz Afikei Kinneret a few more years, uncertain of their future, undecided about whether to leave or stay. The inertia of daily life and its cycles – work, the initial years of parenting, visits to Motti and Rivka, occasional greetings from Bora, letters and phone calls from overseas family, holidays at the beach – kept them going. Joe served as a reserve soldier about a month every year. Training, guard duty, patrols, convoys and then... Jenny started her nursing studies.

June 1982. He was called up with his reserve infantry unit to participate in the first war in Lebanon. It was a controversial war. Many were opposed, but Joe went reluctantly, full of doubts, but happy to join his mates again. They were revved up for the crossing north but full of fear. He'd never seen real action, nor had most of his buddies.

And then, on the way north into Lebanon he was wounded. A piece of shrapnel in his shoulder.

He recovered, apart from nights sometimes returning to the scene, waking in a pool of sweat. He would relive again the moment of the explosion, the rotten eggs smell of the explosive, then lift his head again to see his friend Amos on the road, motionless in his blood, his hand severed beside him, then again hear the loud thrumming of the helicopter overhead and its landing thwump thwump, and feel again the sudden sharp pain in his shoulder as they carried him bouncing on the stretcher behind Amos on his. He awoke in the hospital, Amos was gone.

It happened on the eastern front, opposite the Syrians, just beyond Bint Jbeil.

Joe called Jenny from the hospital in Safed the next morning after the doctors' rounds.

"Jen, I'll be home soon," he yelled cheerfully into the kibbutz dining room phone. "Kiss Rina for me, tell everyone I'm OK!"

"What happened, Joe?"

"A little gift from the enemy. They're pulling it out of my

shoulder soon. It's a minor operation."

"Oh my God! What! How?"

"A bomb, a trap set up at a curve in the road winding through their pretty mountains, then sniper fire. Only one guy, Amos, was badly hurt, no one killed, but he lost his hand, poor guy. We didn't see them. They got away, the bastards."

"Thank God you weren't killed. I'll take time off work for the next couple of days. I'm coming."

Jenny convinced Nachshon, with Selma's help, to drive her down to Tiberias that same afternoon and she just managed to catch the last bus to Safed. She walked the narrow streets of this dusty city of mystics and artists as the last light faded, until she reached the hospital at the bottom of the hill. It was already evening when she arrived at the hospital and found Joe's room. He was lying there after his left shoulder had been operated on, dozing when she walked in. His shoulder was packed in bandages, his left wrist attached to a bottle of fluid on a stand.

"Wohooh, look at you, Mr. soldier hero, sir! All bandaged and tubed up. That's a pain killer in that bottle?"

"Jenny, you've managed to get here so fast! How did you do it? Eh... Yes, morphine, and antibiotics."

"Nachshon drove me down to Tiberias... Here, this is from your daughter! Rina misses you. Selma, Dov and everyone send their love, too."

She gave him a drawing filled with hearts and flowers, *Daddy, come home soon* written across the bottom and signed *Rina* in his little girl's scrawly handwriting. Joe was embarrassed to feel a tear rolling down his cheek. Jenny wiped it away, to his annoyance.

I'm not a baby! But she is being sweet...

"It's so good to see you again, Jen. Sorry I look like this, but I'll be on the mend in no time. They promised me a speedy recovery, told me how lucky I am. My friend Amos wasn't so lucky."

"Joe, you should try to rest. I'm staying overnight. Selma's taking care of Rina. Get some sleep."

They kissed, Jenny sitting on the chair next to him, her hand caressing his good shoulder. Joe, drugged up and exhausted, soon fell asleep.

She spent the next two nights in the hospital beside him. They removed the morphine the next day, gave him antibiotics to take orally and he was already walking around that afternoon. She saw it wasn't serious and decided she had to return to the kibbutz.

What an angel Jenny is! Better than any of the nurses here. I wish she could stay but Rina, and her patients, need her. I'll find Amos and keep him company until I'm released home. The poor bugger lost his hand but at least he's alive.

When Jenny was ready to go, they hugged, he promised to "be good", asked her to bring Rina a gift "from Daddy" and then she left. His heart sank when she did. He went back to obsessing about what had happened. He went looking for Amos in the other rooms, but he wasn't anywhere; the senior orthopaedics nurse told him he had been transferred to Rambam Hospital in Haifa, that they weren't able to save his hand, were dealing with a serious infection and shellshock. He was in a psychiatric ward there. Joe called, but Amos didn't want to talk.

Alone again.

Jenny knew Joe would get lonely. She called and told Rivka and Motti. Rivka came to visit right away bringing him chocolates, but Motti had to stay home, recuperating from another minor heart attack. Joe was sorry he wasn't well, missed his wise counsel and sent him speedy recovery greetings with Rivka.

Bora soon contacted Jenny, concerned. He visited Joe in the hospital, which Joe appreciated. It was a strange, awkward visit. He told Joe how much he admired Ariel Sharon, that it was good he had kicked the PLO out of Beirut. Joe got angry, said he had his doubts about Sharon, felt they had been lied to about the aims of this war, told Bora about the anger of so many of the soldiers in his unit who thought it was not a war of defence, perhaps had been unnecessary, that too many had died.

"Using such massive force against civilians to catch a few terrorists, besieging Beirut, it was crazy!" Joe said.

"It was what had to be done," Bora answered.

"Maybe, but it was like trying to swat a fly with a house!"

Bora laughed, then broke into a lingering, patronizing smile.

"You are still young, Yossi. One day you will understand."

They argued until Joe realized that there was no use doing so. He didn't tell Bora he was considering joining the protest movement against the Lebanon war. Bora would not understand.

He returned to the kibbutz, went back to work, nursing his sore shoulder for many more months; he didn't join the city demonstrations, though he sympathized with them.

Bora later invited them to visit at Beit Alfa, to meet his wife, but they never found the time to do so. Jenny dutifully answered his annual New Year greeting, but otherwise Joe continued to keep his distance. He didn't know why but there was a growing resentment in him at the man.

They had a second child, a boy, Eitan. They invited Bora to the Brit (circumcision ceremony) but he didn't come, sent an apology from overseas.

Jenny completed her nursing qualification. Joe became an agricultural advisor for the kibbutz movement.

They stopped hearing from Bora.

Joe left the old coat in the boydem storage space. One day Rina climbed up into the boydem and pulled the coat down to play with it. But Jenny put it back up without telling Joe. She knew Joe loved that coat and was hesitant to throw away the old thing, however much she wanted him to do just that. He had forgotten about it. She would have thrown it away herself, finally got rid of it... but she too forgot about it.

It waited in the boydem to be remembered.

Part 3
TO RUSSIA AND BACK

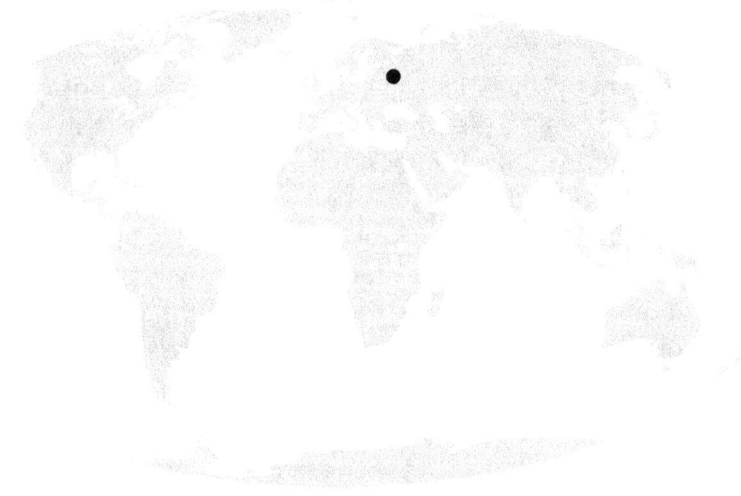

Chapter 24

"Bring the Coat"
Bora Again: 1985

Selma, now the kibbutz manager, told Joe after work one afternoon, "There's a message for you in the kibbutz office."

"A message?"

"Yes. Some guy called and asked me to write down his name and phone number and said something I didn't understand. I wrote it all down."

"All right. So can you give me the key and I'll go get it. Where is it?"

"You know where I always leave notes – on the notice board behind the desk – it's pinned up there. I wrote it in red ink. You'll see it. And it's not locked, just go in and take it."

"OK. Thanks, Selma."

Joe walked out the back of the kitchen through the pantry and across to the little wooden hut that served as an office for the young kibbutz. He saw the red note right away, unpinned and opened it.

Joseph Borowski – call Kibbutz Beit Alfa, 04-77785. Urgent! Call him before he leaves for overseas on Sunday week. Arrange to meet him at Beit Alfa. As soon as possible. Any day this week. Bring the old fur coat with you.

Why does he suddenly want the coat now? He told me it brings back bad memories.

So, he called:

"Hello, Bora?"

"Yes, Yossi. I'm happy you called. Please come meet me at my kibbutz as soon as you can. It's urgent."

"What's this all about? Why?"

"Don't ask questions. Just come and bring my old coat with you please."

"No explanations? Why should I come? You're just giving

190

me an order? I'm not one of your agents!"

"I know that. I can't explain on the phone. You've got to come. I'll make it worth your while."

Silence...

"All right. I'll talk to Jenny and then get back to you."

"Just leave me a recorded message in the kibbutz office whether you are coming or not – within the next 24 hours."

The phone line clicked closed... Bora was gone.

That's it? What's this all about? He's long retired… Why all the sudden pressure to go meet him? And that old coat back now? I don't remember where it is anymore… Ah, in the boydem… it's up there, I think. Jenny would know.

"Guess who called me, Jenny, after all these years?"

"Bora?"

"Yes. He wants me to come, to meet him at Beit Alfa in the next couple of days, urgently. Didn't give me any explanation, just said to bring the old coat with me."

"That's it? Strange."

"Yes. Not sure what to do with this. Why all the sudden urgency when I haven't heard from him in years?"

Jenny was smiling mischievously.

"So, are you going to meet him? I think you should."

"We have a new baby, I have work, why should I go?"

"Just a hunch, Joe. Call it a woman's intuition if you like. I'll manage. Selma is always there to help. Why don't you just take the day off tomorrow and go find out what he wants this time. You need an outing."

"You know what, Jen. I will. Just for the adventure. I'm curious."

Early the next morning, having left a phone message the evening before, Joe kissed a half-sleeping Jenny and headed for the kibbutz car. It was still dark, but he could drive down the snake path with his eyes closed, having travelled that route so often. The Tnuva delivery truck passed going the other way, just beyond the kibbutz wheat fields. Then he was alone on the road. He wondered about Bora's strange request. He remembered to bring the old fur coat. It lay beside him curled up like a sleeping cat, its secrets hidden in its folds. Maybe Bora changed his mind and now wanted it back?

The first soft light of dawn appeared between the hills as he descended from the plateau into the Jordan Valley. Another vehicle, an army jeep, passed him, dipping its lights and again he was solitary on his way to Beit Alfa. As he drove out into the Kinneret basin, the sun appeared through the banana trees on his right, its light shimmering on the lake.

An hour later he drove through Beit She'an out into the now green Jezreel Valley, turned into a side road at the Beit Alfa sign, and up to the gates of the old kibbutz. He passed two tractors on their way out to the fields as he drove in. The guard at the gate greeted Joe and, on hearing the name Joseph Borowski, waved him in.

Bora opened the door. He was wearing a blue dressing gown.

"Ah, Yossi! I knew you would come. Good to see you."

The same ironic smile, mischievous eyes and powerful handshake, the scarred face, the limp.

"Take a seat. Here, sit down in the shade of our grapevine. Shifra will soon bring out drinks, then we shall talk. I see you brought the coat. Very good, very good. Put it down over there."

Joe was surprised to find Bora so talkative. He placed the coat on the wooden bench Bora pointed to and sat down on a wicker chair under an awning of twisted vine branches and vine leaves. Bora lowered himself into a large rocking chair opposite him.

A short, dark, wiry woman, wearing blue work clothes and an orange apron, appeared at the edge of the patio, glanced at Bora for permission to enter. He nodded. She managed a slight shy smile as she brought them a pitcher of lemonade and two glasses. Joe smiled back. Bora's eyes spoke impatience.

"I'm Joe Kamens, my wife, Jenny, and I live up in the Golan Heights, in Afikei Kinneret. It's a pleasure to meet you, Mrs. Borowski."

Bora was now waving at her to leave.

"Yes, I know who you are. You've been here before to meet Bora. Nice to see you again, Yossi. Make yourself at home. I'm sure my husband will take good care of you. I must leave now for a meeting of the Culture committee. There's cake on the kitchen table."

She glared at her husband and left.

He sighed.

"So, Yossi, now that we are here alone, I want to get straight to business."

"Business? What business?"

"I'm leaving for the Soviet Union this coming Sunday. I'd like you to join me. This is a mission of national importance. The Communist system is beginning to weaken. We have an opportunity to encourage Jews there to reconnect with the Jewish people again, and perhaps leave. I'm sure you've heard of their new secretary general, Gorbachev, and his internal policy of Glosnost, his interest in a detente with the USA, right?"

This is crazy! I don't believe him. He looks so old now, but wants to go over to Russia and take me with him? Just get up and go like that? He's got to be kidding.

"Wait a minute Bora! Not so fast. Yes, I know things are changing in Russia but what does that have to do with me? I can't just get up and drop everything and join you. We have a young child and a baby. I have my work, and anyway I already told you years ago that I'm not interested in getting involved in the Mossad. And... why did you ask me to bring your old coat?"

"One thing at a time, Yossi. No one is asking you to work for the Mossad this time. I've retired, as you know. This is a project of Nativ, a clandestine organization helping Soviet Jews."

Joe shifted uncomfortably on his chair, waiting impatiently.

What's the coat got to do with this?

"I've been advising them for years now. We have been secretly supplying Russian Jews with prayer books, textbooks for learning Hebrew, and news from the outside. Our activists also bring back new information about the prisoners of Zion."

"I've been following that in the news, Bora. I know there are

193

Jews sitting in jail over there for teaching Hebrew, requesting to immigrate to Israel. Whatshername... Avital Sharansky... she's in the news all the time... campaigning for her husband's release."

"I heard you're interested."

Joe stared at him suspiciously.

"I have my sources. In any case, your record in the I.D.F. was excellent. You were recommended for Mossad work. Your Australian passport would be very useful in this matter. I know we can rely on you to be of help."

"But what about the coat? Why did you have me bring the coat today?"

"Bring it over here. Let me show you something."

Joe brought the coat over to him. Bora produced a pair of scissors from his dressing gown pocket and spread the coat open on his lap. He began cutting the inside seam.

Joe watched incredulous as Bora opened a large, long slit, pushed his hand in behind the fur lining and pulled out a cloth package from which he withdrew a wrinkled brown envelope. He tore it open and pulled out a small black and white photo of a young woman, and a sheet of paper covered in Yiddish handwriting.

Bora whispered to himself in Russian, as he struggled to control himself, then he looked up at Joe, pain in his eyes.

I've never seen him like this before. What's going on? He's so emotional...

"You're shocked?"

"Yes... but, but I never felt anything inside there... and... who is that a picture of? Why haven't you been interested in the coat before this! I've had it for years now!"

"This is a picture of my sister, Sonia."

Bora's voice cracked as he spoke. He paused, struggling for the words, but he continued: "The is a letter she sent me from the Vilna Ghetto. I thought I had lost it. Then, recently, one night, I remembered where it was. The letter tells of the fate of the Jews there. I had it sewn into the coat to protect it from damage during the years in the forest. It was all I had left of my family after the massacres. I suppose I repressed the memory because it was so painful for me. In any case, that is not the only reason I wanted the coat."

Ah, now he sounds like the Bora I know! He's got his composure back and is in control again, has a plan."

"No? What else?"

"Remembering how I used the coat as a safe hiding place for something so valuable to me gave me an idea for the coming trip to Russia. The coat could be a very useful way to carry material to Soviet Jewish activists over there."

"That's clever. Of course, you can take it back and use it that way."

"No, No, Yossi. I want you to join me, and I want you to keep the coat, and I must tell you that I am deeply grateful to you for having preserved the coat these many years and that you brought it to me with its hidden treasure inside, but the coat will continue to be of use now."

Bora kissed the photo, folded the page with the photo in it back into the envelope, and slid it into his shirt pocket as they spoke.

A long silence, Bora waiting.

He's helped me a lot over the years in his weird way. This might be my opportunity to make amends for disappointing him in the past, a way of showing him my appreciation.

"OK. I'll come."

"Good boy!"

He, of course, discussed all this with Jenny as soon as he got back that evening.

"What an amazing story," Jenny said. "Who would have guessed the coat contained such a precious family treasure. Joe, I think this is an important, even noble, project to be part of. You need a change of scenery and, who knows, it might lead to an opportunity you'd otherwise miss. Bora's not getting younger, you know."

"But how can I just go off to galivant around in Russia and leave you to deal with the kids?"

But I think she's right. It's a once in a lifetime opportunity to do something big. If she's OK with it, I'll go.

"I'll manage and I'm sure Selma will help with the kids," she said.

The kibbutz had no objection to his trip. And so, the next Tuesday, Joe, wearing the partisan coat, lining stuffed with educational material for Russian Jews, boarded a plane from Tel Aviv to Vienna, and from there changed to a flight to Moscow.

Bora met him at the Moscow airport...

■■■

Bora and Joe sat in the train to Minsk from Leningrad. They were both silent, as were the other two people in their cubicle. One, a bent old man with thick glasses and a shiny bald head, was reading a newspaper. Beside him sat a woman who looked about fifty years old. She stared out the window. They both wore simple peasant attire.

The experience in Moscow of being followed everywhere was still fresh in Joe's mind.

They don't look suspicious to me, but you can't be sure. I must be careful what I say. You never know who might be a KGB agent here.

He sat silently across from Bora, who was reading a Soviet newspaper, the page with its Cyrillic words bouncing up and down with the motion of the locomotive. The two prayer books he carried were sewn into his coat, as were some Hebrew language instruction pamphlets. He was nervous that they might be discovered. He felt the unusual bulk of the opened-out books under his arm. He couldn't feel the pamphlets in the fur lining, but he could feel the prayer books. Their corners dug into his inner arms, jabbing him as the train moved. The thought of a possible arrest and of spending time in a Russian jail terrified him. He had heard stories from others who had come to the Soviet Union on similar missions. Some were detained, had materials confiscated, were roughed up and had been expelled. It could be worse. He might not be so lucky. Though it was very cold, he was sweating. Fear.

People have been assassinated in this country, some simply disappeared.

Nothing in his life, growing up in Melbourne, his kibbutz life, or his army service, had prepared him for this challenge. He had never felt this kind of anxiety before. Bora's experience and presence were reassuring, sure, but Joe thought his mentor looked suspicious with his scarred face and hands, despite his limp and walking stick. On the other hand, so many of the older people they had met along the way were war invalids of one kind or another, missing an arm or a leg, as well as their facial scars. There were plenty of those. Maybe they would be OK, as Bora assured him. True, they had come this far without any direct interaction with the police or the KGB, but there was no certainty that there might not be now or in Minsk.

Just like in Moscow, there might be a hidden camera in the hotel room where we will stay. Bora's so aware of their techniques to watch us. I am glad he pointed out the camera. They're probably keeping an eye on us now too.

Looking out the window, he saw rows of thin birch trees. Like soldiers guarding the train's passageway, they stood erect and silent as the train sped through the vast Belorussian Forest. The train stopped at a small country station, surrounded by forest. Joe squinted, trying to read the station's name, but it was too faded to decipher. The two other passengers disembarked, leaving Joe and Bora the only ones to get back on train from the wooden platform. The train creaked, groaned, and moved on again.

"It was in a forest like this that I fought as a partisan during *the Great Patriotic War*," Bora commented, his voice tinged with sarcasm as he pronounced the title.

Joe furrowed his brows. "Oh. But the trees are so thin. Couldn't you have been seen by the Germans in there. You attacked the German trains and went into villages all the time? Didn't they follow you into the forest? Weren't you in constant danger? How could you do it?"

Bora leaned back; his face sombre: "You don't understand, Yossi. The forest covers forty percent of Belarus; it's immense.

197

We controlled it, and the Germans were afraid to enter without a massive force.

When they did, we retreated into the swamps, only to return when they withdrew."

"It must have been a life of continuous fear. What kept you going?"

"We had nothing to lose. After the massacres of the Jews, and thousands of Soviet prisoners of war, we felt as if we were already dead men. We wanted revenge, to kill as many fascists as we could. What we're doing now is a picnic compared to those years."

Joe nodded, trying to grasp the weight of those experiences. "I think I get it."

Bora's eyes softened, and he smiled sadly. "But there were good times as well, sitting around a campfire singing, drinking vodka, as the Germans began to retreat. I still remember the words of our favourite Russian song – *Ochi chyornye* about love of a gypsy woman."

Bora sang a few bars, his deep voice off-key, then stopped abruptly, his expression bitter. "We sometimes sang songs in Yiddish too."

As they arrived in Minsk, two elderly women met them at the station and escorted them to a small hotel. The lobby was large, high-ceilinged, poorly lit, and devoid of any other human presence. A portrait of Lenin hung on the wall opposite Joe, while a few low glass tables and green upholstered chairs filled the room.

Joe heard a cough behind him. A suspicious-looking lady receptionist with Asian features and red eyes greeted them with an artificial smile. After signing in at the desk and leaving their documents, they proceeded to their room. Joe noticed that Bora had supplied the woman with a Russian passport (probably forged) along with his own (very real) Australian passport, which made Joe nervous.

"Get some sleep, Yossi. We have a busy day ahead of us tomorrow," Bora said.

"What's the agenda?"

Bora lowered his voice to say, "Well, after breakfast we will again be escorted by a Soviet 'In-tourist' travel guide as we were in Moscow and Leningrad." He winked at Joe meaningfully. "The guide will take us to the Soviet War Museum here, and then we'll have a tour of the city to see the sites of major battles and other war memorials. Later we will dine with some local "Communist officials", among whom there will be a man we want to give materials to... I'll point him out to you, but it should be obvious as he'll be wearing a coat similar to yours. His name is Sasha. You'll give him your coat and take his."

Joe scratched his head and asked, "The coat? Won't there be heating where we meet?"

"Of course. You'll swap coats as we leave. Don't worry. You will get your beloved coat back – later – with something else in the lining replacing what we've brought them," Bora explained.

The next morning, in the hotel lobby, after a sparse breakfast of tasteless coffee, toast, hard boiled eggs, and a slice of pickled cucumber each, they met their guide, Vladimir. He was a big man, with large red ears, a shaved head, and a huge smile. His blue eyes were shining, merry.

"Welcome to Minsk! You will spend the day with me seeing the sites of our glorious resistance, and our victory over the Fascists in the Great War of the Homeland, a lunch with some local Party officials. The highlight will be to visit our UNESCO-recognized War Museum. It is one of the wonders of the world, complete with authentic artifacts from that time."

He shook their hands with an iron grip.

"Nice to meet you," Joe said after recovering his squeezed hand.

"Yes, we know the itinerary. Lead the way," said Bora, as their giant guide hovered over them.

"I know you are from Israel, though you came in on foreign passports, and that is OK with us now," the man told them. "The government has instructed us to be welcoming to Jewish visitors. You should know we have equal rights for all in our

Communist regime here. The stories about persecution of Jews are American capitalist propaganda. Lies."

"I have heard. You believe in detente, right?" Bora asked cynically.

"Ah, yes! You know about our new policies."

Joe, who had remained silent, wondered about this man.

Could he have been a wrestler, or a basketball player, for the Soviet Union? He looks the type.

"Yes!" Vladimir seemed to read Joe's mind when he said, "I have been overseas many times to represent the Soviet Union in the Olympic games."

"Which sport?" Joe finally managed to ask.

Vladimir turned to face him. "Shot-put. I won silver twice in Moscow in 1980, and in Los Angeles last year. I know English well, as you can hear, but have never met Israelis before. Why do you look surprised? We know all about you and your mission here."

Joe and Bora looked at each other, but neither responded.

Vladimir laughed. "Follow me. I will show you some local hospitality!"

They walked out of the lobby, following behind him.

Vladimir took them for a tour of the city in his Moskvitch kombi hatchback. "My car is the newest in Russian automobiles," he told them. They travelled along the Svislach river, including a visit to an island called the "Island of Tears", where a monument was being built in memory of the soldiers who'd died in the Afghanistan war, a descent into the new underground metro recently built, and a visit to the MT2 factory where tractors were assembled for export throughout the Soviet "empire."

They ended the tour, Joe exhausted, at a gigantic statue of Lenin standing atop a monstrous black plinth in Lenin Square. Next, they headed to a nearby "French" restaurant.

Joe was impressed with Bora's stamina, who, despite his limp, with the use of his solid olivewood walking stick, managed to keep up with Vladimir's pace, Joe often lagging behind.

Vladimir expressed pride in his city's recent history. He

explained that it had, after being a centre of anti-Fascist resistance, recovered from almost total destruction in the second world war to become one of the most important industrial and administrative centres of Communist rule.

Vladimir told them, "Eighty percent of the city was destroyed!"

It was only as they entered the "Le Monde" restaurant on the far side of the square that Bora mentioned to Vladimir that he too had lived in Minsk – in 1944-5 – after the partisan forces and the Red Army had met there and expelled the Germans.

"Why did you leave? Stalin?"

"Yes, Stalin."

They entered the dimly lit restaurant, walked past a bar along which sat some working men drinking what looked like vodka, and followed Vladimir and their waiter into a back room. Vladimir had to stoop to get through the entrance as they came in.

There, they were seated at a round table already set for six places.

"Your friends will be here soon," Vladimir informed them. "I will return in 55 minutes. Enjoy your meal!" He grabbed a glass and downed a shot of vodka.

"LeHaim!" he said. "You should know I am Ivri too," he added, laughing.

As Vladimir left, stooping to go out, four dour, unsmiling men entered the room, greeting Vladimir curtly as they passed him. They peeled off their outer garments and hung them on the clothes rack, as Joe and Bora had done earlier. The first three older men to enter the room were all bald, grey, and wrinkled below their fur hats, the fourth, a bit younger, had a bushy head of hair which he freed from under his hat. He took off a fur coat that looked almost identical to Joe's. He hung it beside Joe's. They sat down at the table.

"You are Borowski?" one of them asked, as he wiped steam off his glasses. He had a white chin beard like Lenin's in the photos seen during their tour earlier in the day.

"Da."

Bora spoke to them in fluent Russian, Joe understanding nothing. The conversation was intense. The Lenin-like beard jutted forward aggressively as he spoke, retreating into his neck as he listened. The others remained silent, eyeing Bora, then Joe, occasionally nodding in agreement. The younger one with the head of hair spoke up.

"Your friend here does not know Russian?"

"None," Bora admitted.

"Then let us speak English, and perhaps it is now time for a toast to the future of our Soviet-Israel relations – once we have a peace agreement in the Middle East."

Joe was surprised by this sudden proposed toast, considering the lack of formal diplomatic relations between the two countries. Bora looked relaxed, not at all surprised at his words, as the man poured each a glass of vodka.

"To our future relations!"

"But I thought we were here to speak of scientific matters..." Joe whispered to Bora.

"That was just a cover. These gentlemen are friends of ours, working for rapprochement between our peoples. This is Sasha..." he whispered, indicating the younger man to Joe.

"Ah, young man, let me explain something to you," the bearded one said, turning to Joe. "We know you are here to help the local Jews. We are in favour of immigration of those who want to move to Israel, but we need some diplomatic progress first, and your friend Borowksi will help us with that. He and I were comrades-in-arms in the same partisan unit, under Colonel Markov, and we have maintained contact for many years since. He has important connections in your country, and now is the time to use them."

They refilled their glasses and downed a second, and then a third shot of vodka. The steaming borscht soon arrived. They were all smiling now. Joe was having trouble sitting straight as the alcohol turned his head.

Sasha wanted to know more. "Joe, tell me about you and your country..."

"I live on a kibbutz, a new one in the Golan Heights."

"A kolhoz in occupied territory?"

"Yes, I suppose so. But it is a strategic place, conquered from the Syrians at a great cost."

"That's all very well, but once there is a peace agreement, you will have to move, to return to your own country. Anyway, tell me more about the life there. I am curious."

Joe described the daily routine on his kibbutz, the fortnightly members' meetings, the committees, the arguments over shared television, the children's house. His new "friend" listened with great interest.

"It is a pity you will have to move, but one must make sacrifices for the sake of peace," Sasha commented.

Bora glared at him momentarily, lifted a finger to his mouth in warning to Joe, as if to say, "be careful what you say!"

Joe didn't believe there would ever be peace with the Arabs. His was just a theoretical agreement to oblige. He felt this was a game they were playing but didn't understand why.

The men got up to leave. As they put their coats on, the bearded one turned back to face Bora and said something in Russian. Joe saw that Sasha had taken his coat and left the one he had worn hanging there.

"What did that guy say, Bora?"

"He said, 'See you in Tel Aviv, and be careful until you leave our country; not everyone approves of our conversation here.'"

Joe put on his "new" coat, and he and Bora left the restaurant.

When they returned, exhausted, to the hotel, Bora invited Joe to stop at the bar for an early "nightcap." They sat at one of the low tables, drinking beer, and recalling the day's events: the visit to the museum where he had seen, to his amazement, the very same fur coat again, on display in the partisan warfare section, the strange lunch conversation, and Vladimir's proud revelation of his ethnic origin. It was there in the museum that he remembered how he had first discovered the coat as a child in Melbourne.

Vladimir suddenly appeared and came over to them carrying a big parcel wrapped in brown paper. He placed it on Joe's lap and whispered... "Here's your coat. There's something important sewn inside, but please don't touch it until you get home, OK?"

Joe nodded, feeling a sense of mission the coat had created in his life, staring at the parcel.

What a journey this coat and I have had together!

They stood to bid farewell to Vladimir, and he gave each of them a bearhug and left.

"But what about the other coat?"

"Don't worry about that. Just leave it behind in the room. It will be taken care of."

■■■

When they returned to Tel Aviv, Bora took the coat from Joe. He cut open the lining under one sleeve and pulled out an envelope.

"It's a list of names," Bora explained.

Joe was baffled, but then thought to ask... "Is Vladimir on that list?"

"Yes. He already has a sister here. Sasha, the man you spoke with at our meeting in Minsk, you remember, he's also listed."

"Oh, yes. I guessed. He looked Jewish."

"You did a big mitzvah, Yossi. You will understand just how big in a few years, I'm sure. This was a window of opportunity that might only be open briefly."

Joe felt grateful to Bora for having involved him, but he came home to his family unnerved by the strange experience. He limited what he told Jenny and the others about the trip to the Soviet Union as he'd promised Bora.

He felt he'd witnessed something important, perhaps historic, but wondered why Bora had needed him there. His role, to be honest, had been minimal. Was he there to be a witness to Bora's secret negotiations? He and Bora never spoke about it again. There was no debriefing; he returned to a state of limited contact with him, and then Bora again disappeared from his life.

When Natan Sharansky was released a year later, and

allowed to immigrate to Israel, Joe and Jenny watched the events unfold on television with bated breath. The drama on the Berlin tarmac left them both in tears. Sharansky refused to leave the plane until he was given back his book of Psalms, the worn little book that had accompanied him in solitary confinement in the Gulag prison, the one he had received from his new bride Avital, before being incarcerated. Joe noticed the man was wearing a familiar fur coat when he first emerged from the Soviet plane.

"A brave and stubborn man."

"Yes, and you know I contributed something to that, Jenny."

"How?"

"One of the books I smuggled into Moscow was for him."

Chapter 25

A VISIT TO FRIENDS

In the autumn of 1987, their old friends Hanoch and Tamar, now a family of nine souls, invited Joe and Jenny to join them for the festival of Sukkot in Kedumim in the northern West Bank.

Joe had his doubts about going, knowing that the journey was dangerous. Nor was he enthusiastic about encouraging his childhood friend's crazy religious and nationalist fanaticism. It was Jenny who was excited about going, insisted that they should accept their friends' invitation to spend the festival with them.

"Remember their wedding there? It was so joyful and special! Nothing bad happened on the way there that time or when we drove there twice after that for their sons' circumcisions. I don't understand why we've seen them so seldom over the past few years."

"Their fanaticism, Jenny. One of these days they will be attacked for plonking themselves there amongst all those Arabs and lording it over them all the time. If it wasn't for the army, they wouldn't last there a day!"

"But he was a good friend of yours for so long, a childhood buddy. You don't have many people like that in the country today. You should be more considerate, Joe. I think we should go."

"Oh, all right. I suppose we should go."

As an agricultural advisor now, Joe often had use of the kibbutz cars, particularly the blue Peugeot station wagon donated the previous year by a Canadian millionaire, a friend of Steve's. He arranged use of the car, scheduling some visits on the way to a couple of new agricultural settlements in the Jordan Valley, just south of Beit She'an.

Jenny packed some sandwiches; he prepared a thermos of tea. They carried their bulging overnight bags out to the car and set off. They had decided not to take the kids this time, leaving them with friends on the kibbutz with kids the same age as theirs. Rina and Eitan loved to play with them most days after school and were happy to spend more time with their best playmates.

Joe and Jenny set off on this journey, like the young couple they'd once been, pre-kids. It felt like a new adventure.

Down the snake path they drove, past where the burnt-out tractor had once been, along the now rusting barbed wire fence with those danger signs (one with a graffiti of skull and cross bones!) warning of old Syrian mines. They drove past rows of banana plants near the Kinneret shore.

Joe turned at the Tzemach "intersection" where he and Jenny as soldiers on leave had spent many long hours waiting for rides up to the kibbutz, and where they had first become a couple. He turned left, drove past the Jordan Valley kibbutzim – Afikim, Ashdot Yaacov Alef, Ashdot Yaacov Bet, Hamadia, and others, until they began the descent down into the Beit She'an Valley.

It was late October. Although it had already rained, it was hot again, a hamsin. They had the air-conditioning on full blast, and the radio on Galei Zahal, the army radio station. They heard a song about unrequited love, Matti Caspi's sweet soft voice that Jenny so loved.

Joe was surprised when Jenny suddenly turned the radio off.

"Why did you do that?"

"I want to talk to you about something, Joe."

"Now? Here?"

"As good a time and place as any I think."

She sounded determined.

"What's up?"

"I want to leave the kibbutz."

"What? Why? Something happened?"

"No. Nothing's happened. We've talked about this before Joe. It's time to move… time to get on with our lives. We're vegetating on Afikei Kinneret."

"Yes. Haven't I said similar things to you in the past?"

"You have, but nothing happened. I'm serious this time. A

new school year just started. The kids are getting more and more rooted in Afikei Kinneret. It's an isolated community. Far away from everywhere. It's going to get harder and harder to move."

"I guess you're right about that, but I'm finally OK with my work now that I can travel around a bit. And I thought you were happy in your work, running the infirmary and being school nurse down in Ein Gev. And the kids are happy too, aren't they?"

"You're wrong Joe! They're not happy in the school, you just don't notice. Ever since you went to Russia with Bora you've become more distant. What's bugging you?"

"I don't know. I guess you're right that I'm not always with it, that I spend a lot of time reading and thinking about politics and what's happening in the country, and not enough time with the kids."

"Yeah. You said it! Rina isn't happy, she's bored in school. The school in Ein Gev is awful, educationally, and the older kids in the kibbutzim around here are getting into drugs because of the foreign volunteers. That scares me. And Eitan... yes, he's a naturally happy child, sings to himself while playing with his Lego, but he suffers from the violence on the school playground. He's such a sensitive kid..."

"Oh... Yes, you've told me about that, but I thought those are just normal kid problems..."

"And as for me, Joe... you haven't noticed, have you... you don't know!? I'm frustrated, and bored. I need a change. You have your little agricultural excursions to other kibbutzim, your political involvement, but I'm stuck on Afikei Kinneret and the Ein Gev primary school, day after day. I want to move already."

"It's not so simple. There's a lot involved."

"Joe, if *we* don't move, I will."

Joe suddenly stopped the car on the side of the road.

"You're threatening to leave me?"

"Joe, Joe... you know I love you, but we only have one life, and I don't see things getting any better if we stay on the kibbutz."

"But how could you say that! Of course, you're more important to me than anything else. If you're unhappy... but I had no idea you were so desperate for a change. I need a change too, and I want what's best for you and the kids. We'll move, but it'll take time. You should be patient a little longer. Please, Jenny."

"How long? What do you mean?"

Joe explained... "We need a plan. We have to choose where to live, find jobs, a high school for Rina, and a new elementary school for Eitan. He'll need a special one, something experimental, democratic you know. We've got to prepare the kids for such big changes in their lives… We can't just suddenly uproot the family."

Jenny turned towards Joe, grabbed his arm, and said... "I have an idea. You'll contact Bora. He's a smart guy and he has connections. I'm sure he'd be willing to help us relocate."

Joe looked at Jenny sceptically: "Bora? We haven't heard from him in a while. He must be very old by now. Is he even still alive?"

Jenny was getting enthusiastic as she spoke. "Rivka's in contact with him and told me he's as vigorous as always, that he's now writing a book. I'm sure we could contact him through her, if you don't have the number from your trip to Russia with him. You know how much she loves us and has enjoyed doting on our kids, when we visit her, especially since she became a widow."

"Yeah, good idea… it's time we visited her again. Maybe we could speak to her first to get her advice... she's so committed to kibbutz life… Would you consider living on another kibbutz, one more central, less isolated than Afikei Kinneret?"

"I don't know. If it's a bigger place and more central... Maybe, but I would rather the city, honestly."

"OK Jenny, we'll check out some possible directions. I'll ask her to help."

Joe started the car again. He switched off the double warning lights and was strapping on his safety belt when a police car pulled over beside them. A long, thin, and dark face wearing dark-rimmed glasses was staring in at them from the driver's window.

The policeman asked, "Everything OK with you two?"

"Yes, officer. We just pulled over for a short break on the way," Joe answered.

"And where are you from?" he continued.

Joe answered impatiently: "Kibbutz Afikei Kinneret. We're headed to Kedumim to spend the holiday with friends there."

"You'd better be careful, then. There's a hostile Arab population in that area. They don't like visiting Israeli Jews and there have been stone-throwing incidents in the area."

"Thanks for the update on the situation. We'll be careful," Jenny responded.

"Please show me your identity cards now."

Joe dug out their cards. "Sure. Here they are."

The friendly police officer handed the two blue documents over to his partner – a bald, big-bellied policeman still sitting in the police car. He glanced at them, and handed them back, waving to them from inside to get going.

"You can be on your way now, but in future, you ought to find a safer place to pull over for a break. There are accidents here all the time. Cars coming around that curve don't see what's coming and sometimes swerve right here to avoid accidents with oncoming trucks."

As he spoke, a delivery van swerved around the curve, skidding and slowing down as the driver sighted the police car. "See. Just as I said!"

Joe and Jenny both laughed nervously as they took back their documents.

"It's no laughing matter. Move on now. And be careful in the Shomron. Have a good holiday!"

The police car drove off, and they resumed their journey.

As they drove south, the scenery changed; the green of the northern Jordan Valley was gone and the hills were now barren. Shrubs and trees were infrequent in the landscape, then they disappeared altogether. The moon-like landscape outside beyond Beit She'an was familiar to Joe, but not to Jenny.

"How can anyone live in this desert?" she wondered.

Joe breathed deeply, then waved one hand expansively and said, "You'd be surprised. I've learned to love this Land, especially places like this. If there's a God, this is where you could connect with Him."

"Not Him, Joe. God isn't masculine."

"Sorry, Jen. It's just a figure of speech. I remember what Yedidya taught us about Maimonides' concept of the Divine."

"Uh huh, I really loved his teaching. Anyway, I don't like this desolation. I don't find it inspiring. Give me trees, green grass, flowers, any day over this!"

They reached a crossroads just as a dusty petrol station appeared like a mirage in the wilderness. They fuelled up and bought coffee.

Joe realized they'd gone a wrong route, the long way. Looking at the map of the West Bank, he saw that he should have turned west at Beit She'an, and not have continued south along road 90 in the Jordan Valley. They pulled out of the petrol station and headed back the way they'd come, looking for a way west out of the desert.

"Can you read the sign over there, Jen?"

"Yes. It's the moshav community we saw on the map. Mehola. Let's drive in to ask directions."

"Sounds good."

They turned left off the road onto a dusty dirt track. As they drove along, a donkey, laden with heavy cloth bags appeared out of nowhere. It was accompanied by a swarthy boy. His head was wrapped in a black and red kafiya. As he approached, Joe saw that he was wearing tight, torn blue jeans and an army-issue work shirt, marked I.D.F. He was carrying a shovel.

Joe slowed the car to a snail-like crawl.

"*Salaam Aleikum. Marhaba!*" the boy called out to them, his smile reaching from ear to ear, eyes bright with welcome. One front tooth was missing.

"Shalom! *Marhabtein!*" Joe answered, smiling too. "*Atta medaber Ivrit?*" he asked him.

"*Lah…lah ma Bakhki Ibreni. Bahki bas shway Inglizi.*"

"He doesn't speak Hebrew, but he knows a little English." Joe explained to his wife, feeling good that he could use a few words of Arabic, and impress her.

"So, you speak some English?" Jenny asked.

"*Aywah!* How are you?" the boy said, showing off his limited knowledge of English.

Joe saw that Jenny was nervous. She eyed the Bedouin boy warily, then pinched Joe's thigh and whispered, "Joe, Joe… keep going. Don't stop. Don't talk to him. He might be a terrorist…"

"Don't be such a worrier, Jen. He's friendly. And he's just a kid…"

While they were whispering about whether to stop or not, another figure suddenly appeared on the ridge above them. Joe saw his arm raised, then the arc of a projectile coming towards them.

He pressed hard on the accelerator. They shot forward as a huge rock landed with a thump just behind the back of the car, spraying the vehicle with gravel and sand. He needed no convincing. He drove off at full speed, leaving the surprised boy behind, frozen on the spot, staring at the rock on the road.

They sped in through the open gates of Mehola. There was no security guard in sight.

Jenny was shaking; Joe was furious.

He parked the car next to a tractor, just beyond the gates.

An unshaven man in blue work clothes, a kippa hanging over his right ear, came up to them.

"Welcome to Mehola. I'm Hilik. You came in here quite dramatically… I heard your brakes screech. What's the matter? What happened?"

"Shalom Hilik. I'm Joe, and this is my wife, Jenny. We're from Afikei Kinneret."

"Ah, yes. I know the place. What's up?"

"An Arab kid just threw a rock at us," Jenny said.

Hilik scratched his stubbled chin, then thoughtfully said… "You don't say. It's usually quiet around here. We get on fine with our neighbours. It's just some Bedouin kid fooling around. Nothing to get excited about. Calm down." His voice was good-humoured, fatherly.

Joe was not placated at all. "Fooling around? That was a big rock. He could have injured us, caused a bad accident, even killed us!"

Hilik's expression had turned serious. He pointed to a little wooden hut just beyond the tractor where they had parked the car.

"Come into my office here. We will call the army, and while we wait, I'll get you something to drink – cold lemonade, or some strong coffee. Come."

They followed him.

I like this guy. A real salt-of-the-earth type. Just the person to help us now.

He felt Jenny shaking beside him, took her hand as they walked across the yard.

"Why don't you call the police," Joe asked, as they walked into Hilik's office.

Joe noticed that the space was decorated with maps and photos of the area, and of the Dead Sea. A fan was clanking in one corner. He saw two plastic folding chairs next to a table, a small cane rocking chair in the far corner, and a fridge, next to a stool with an electric kettle on it…

"Police? There's no police around here! There's a small army outpost down the road, that's all. They might check things out if I call them but don't hold your breath. Nothing much will happen. The kids will be long gone."

Hilik called the army. Joe couldn't believe his ears: "Hello, Shrulik? … Yes. It's Hilik Cohen from Mehola… I want to report another incident down the road from here… Yes, that's right… Yes, today… about 20 minutes ago… an Arabusch threw stones at a passing car… No… no one was hurt… no… no damage… they're gone… You're not coming? Why not? Oh, I see… Well… OK. Yallah, Bye!"

213

"That's it?" Joe exclaimed.

"That's it. Drink up your coffee. There's nothing more we can do now." Hilik, spoke in that paternal tone again. They sipped their coffee while their host brought out a big, detailed map of the area and spread it out on the table.

"You said you want to get to Kedumim?" He pointed to a spot on the map: "Here."

"Yes. We're invited there for Sukkot," Jenny explained.

Hilik turned serious again: "It's a nice place, Kedumim, but surrounded by Arabs. They're not very friendly round there. Be careful."

Joe looked at the map more closely. It was very detailed. "Can you show us how to get there on this map?"

"Of course. Here look. You drive back down to the main Jordan Valley road, turn left back towards Beit She'an, then drive up this road and turn left again. You'll end up near the Jenin refugee camp. Don't stop near there! Just keep driving and turn south towards Nablus, look for the village of Jit. The road opposite takes you into Kadum village, Kedumim is off a dirt track on a hill next to it. Did you take that in?"

Joe showed Hilik and Jenny the map he had sketched himself while listening to the instructions.

"Yep. Got it. We'd better get going so we can get there before dark. Thank you, Hilik. That was very helpful!"

They drove back to the main road, turned towards Beit She'an and on across the Jezreel Valley.

"It is beautiful here, Joe!"

"Yes, isn't it."

They continued past Beit Alfa, then turned into road 60. The outskirts of Jenin soon appeared ahead of them.

"Joe, I'm scared. Let's not do this. Let's go home!"

"But Jenny, we told them we're coming. They're expecting us. You spoke to Tamar yourself. You're the one who insisted on going!"

"I suppose you're right but look at all those mosque turrets. There are no Jews around here. This isn't Israel anymore."

"Close your eyes. Don't look. We will be there soon, I promise."

She did as he said, pulling her hood over her eyes and curling up into her seat. Joe was nervous as he drove along this unfamiliar road. He turned off the radio so Hebrew would not be heard from their car. He noticed that the cars passing them going into Jenin were older, looked beat up. As they left the city behind, he saw at least two donkeys pass by loaded with things, and countless kafiya-covered heads as well as some galabiya-wearing women walking by the side of the road balancing baskets on their heads.

A tractor chugged past after a while. Then they were alone on the road driving between olive groves and cultivated fields, green vegetable patches, and occasional white stone buildings. They soon saw the red roofs of a settlement in the distance.

"Maybe that's Kedumim," Jenny said hopefully. She had come out from under her hood to look around. "It's beautiful here... so green."

Thump! Thump! Glass crashing. Jenny screamed. Stones had hit the side of the car. Joe sped up away from below the terrace rock wall over which the stones were thrown. Their back window was hit; glass splinters lay all over the back seat.

"Are you all right Jenny?"

"Yes. I'm bleeding a bit, the back of my neck, but I'm OK. It's just a scratch. Thank God we didn't bring the kids, Joe!"

They screeched to a halt at the first army checkpoint they came to. Two armed soldiers in full battle dress approached the car.

"What's up?" one of the soldiers asked.

Joe, restraining his anger exclaimed: "Can't you see!? We've been attacked! Someone smashed the back window of the car. They threw stones at us."

Joe looked at the two soldiers and realized they were only kids. One of them was a lieutenant, the other had sergeant's stripes.

"Where are you headed?" the lieutenant asked, calmly.

"Kedumim," Joe said.

"We'll arrange an escort for you when we get back," the sergeant said. "Wait here."

"Hey, Yoram! Come out here and take care of these people till we get back!" he called out.

"There are a couple of reserve soldiers here," he explained, "They'll take care of you."

A short bald older soldier appeared from behind the tent zipping up his fly and smiling at them stupidly. He was wearing bright green sneakers instead of army boots. A bespectacled tall thin soldier, his pants too short for him, followed him, scratching his head. His dusty boots were red.

"There's been some excitement?" the thin one asked.

Joe had calmed now, the comical duo distracting him from his being upset. "You could say that," he replied, laughing. Jenny didn't laugh.

A jeep pulled up, shooting dust up into the air around them. Joe and Jenny watched as the two regular soldiers got into the vehicle. The lieutenant told the driver to drive fast in the direction that Joe had pointed to. Joe nodded that that was the place. The jeep roared away and soon they heard shooting. Suddenly, they heard an explosion, then another. A cloud of smoke appeared above the hill down the road.

"Tear gas," the bald soldier explained.

Then the jeep returned. "They got away," the sergeant admitted.

The lieutenant added, "We have to write a report before we can take you to Kedumim."

"We're not going to Kedumim," Jenny responded. "We're going home."

Joe didn't argue. After they'd finished with the army and phoned their settler friends to apologize, they drove home in the dark.

The first intifada had started.

Chapter 26
A Visit With Rivka

Joe called Rivka a week later, after the Sukkot holiday. He told her what had happened to them when travelling to visit friends in the West Bank. He also told her that they wanted to leave the kibbutz and were interested in her help. She invited them to come visit her in a couple of days to talk their plans over with her, and that she would be happy to help.

Rivka said she was not surprised, that she knew that Jenny couldn't be happy in such an isolated place. She admitted that she was disappointed, as she had admired their pioneering spirit in living up in the Golan. She said she would be willing to help them out, that she had some good connections.

"Is Bora one of them?" Joe asked her.

"Of course. He's the first person I would turn to."

Joe and Jenny planned a trip during which they would visit her and meet with Bora on the same day. Rivka called them to say Bora would come. They both arranged some vacation time, explaining to their kibbutz friends that they needed a break after their traumatic experiences the day before the Sukkot holiday, that they wanted to spend a day by the sea. Despite the cold and the unusual request, their workplaces understood and readily agreed. Everyone had come to see the damage to the car. It had been "the talk of the town" during the week-long holiday.

Rivka met them at the car park. She had greyed now and was leaning on a walking stick. He was saddened to see the change, that she had aged so since Motti's death last year. But her broad warm smile, her high red cheeks, and bright eyes were still the same!

"Shalom Aleichem! Welcome, welcome!" she exclaimed as the car pulled up. "It's good to see you again!"

"Yes, it has been a long time since we were last here," Jenny said. Joe nodded in agreement. "Motti's funeral was the last time we were here."

There was an awkward silence.

Joe and Jenny got out of the car. They hugged their hostess, and then began to unload the car, freeing the two kids to jump out excitedly and run towards "Safta Rivka", expecting the goodies she always carried in her pockets for them and her friends' kids.

"Here you are! One for you, Rina, and one for you, Eitan! Now come. You know where I live, don't you!" Rina nodded, took her brother's hand, and the two followed as Rivka led the way, limping along the path down towards her room.

Joe and Jenny caught up just as Rivka, like a mother hen, was herding her two little chicks away from an oncoming bicycle and around a corner palm tree. They were all chirping happily. As they went in, Joe noted that, unlike many doorposts on the kibbutz, Rivka's had a mezuzah. He kissed it reverently.

Jenny laughed. "Joking, Joe?"

"No," he said.

Rivka and Jenny both stared at him, and then Rivka asked, "Are you becoming religious as you grow older, Yossi?"

"Not exactly, but I do feel as if I'm entering a holy place whenever we visit you, Rivkalleh."

Rivka smiled, appreciatively, placed her walking stick by the bamboo coat-hanger stand, and collected their coats and hung them up, noticing the old fur coat: "And you still wear that old partisan coat after all these years!?"

"Yes. I love the coat. It connects me with my student days. I stopped wearing it for a few years, but after a trip to cold Russia where it was very warm and useful, I went back to wearing it."

Jenny frowned. Rivka nodded understanding. She then headed into her kitchenette calling behind her, "Make yourselves at home!"

Joe looked around. Now a widow, Rivka had made some changes in her living room. There were more books, many of them Judaica books, and there was new artwork on the wall.

Rivka returned with a tray loaded with goodies, which she placed on the coffee table: a bowl of fruit, a pile of glass plates, some dessert spoons and forks, a small bowl of sweets, and a chocolate cake, already sliced.

They all dug in. The kids filled their pockets with sweets, only stopping when Jenny told them they had had enough. Eitan's face was smeared with chocolate cream. Rina only picked at her slice of cake.

Jenny watched the kids for a while and then said, "Please take this away. They are gorging themselves, and they will be impossible later. So, Rivka, these drawings, you did them?"

"Yes. Ever since Motti died I've found comfort in art. I have joined an art class now, and I am enjoying it."

Rivka turned to Joe and asked, "And so, how are the Kamens these days? I know you're no longer happy on Afikei Kinneret."

"That's right, Rivka. We feel we need a change… You said Bora could help us, that he might come to meet with us," Joe reminded her.

"I thought he could, yes. He promised to come, but he called last night to say he's not feeling well. He invited you to go visit him at Beit Alfa soon. Call him."

"We thought you might advise us about how to leave the kibbutz, where to find a place suitable for a young family."

"I know. I thought about that, made some inquiries for you. I have a friend on Kibbutz Maagan Michael. He told me they need a nurse there, and there is a field school, as well as a developed fish industry. Joe, your degree in Marine Biology was of interest to him. Here…"

Rivka took a note from her bag and handed it to Joe. "It's his contact information. His name is Dov Ben David. He's a doctor. He said you should contact him, and he will do what he can."

Jenny hugged and kissed Rivka. "Thank you. That sounds promising."

Rina stared at them, worried, while Eitan, oblivious, played with a wooden model airplane kit. "What are you talking about?" she asked.

"We'll explain in the car on the way home," Jenny answered.

Despite Jenny's encouragement to do so, Joe didn't call Bora to ask after his health. He didn't feel comfortable about contacting the old man again. Two weeks later, Rivka told them Bora had suffered from a flu, had developed pneumonia but had recovered, though weakened, and that it was OK to call him... Jenny nagged Joe about it for a while but dropped the subject when Joe got irritable. Joe was still uncomfortable about visiting Bora, though he didn't understand what it was that bothered him.

Something about Bora has been bugging me ever since our conversation in the hospital when I was wounded, but I'm not sure what it is. Maybe his admiration for Arik Sharon upset me.

They visited Maagan Michael and met with Dr. Ben David and some other kibbutz members. Jenny was offered a job on the spot; Joe was asked to come in for another interview, but they didn't like the school there. They decided to look for a city solution. They began looking into other possible places, work in the cities. Bora suddenly called to share a phone number of a friend in Netanya who would help them there.

"How did you know we were looking to move?"

"I still have my contacts out there. Think about this carefully, Yossi. Are you sure that you want to leave the kibbutz? It's a big move and probably irreversible. I know they value you and your wife there, and you are protecting the country, sitting in that former Syrian stronghold."

"Thank you, Bora. Jenny and I have thought this through, we know what we want. I'll call your army friend, but I'm not sure whether we're interested."

"Suit yourself. But call if you need my help, OK."

Joe could hear Bora's heavy breathing as they spoke, heard him cough twice. "How's you health?" Joe asked.

"I'll live, if the doctors don't kill me," the old man answered, gruffly.

Then, just a dial tone on the phone, he was gone.

Joe was annoyed. Bora's sudden call and attempt to influence his plans disturbed him, but he wrote down the number. A retired general with a lot of clout, Bora had explained. Jenny reminded him of it several times. Joe finally called.

Bora keeps doing this! Interfering with my life, trying to manoeuvre me towards his goals for me and doing so through subtle manipulations. I want my life to be my own…

But Joe called. The retired general arranged an interview with another ex-officer in the I.D.F. who offered him a job teaching high school biology in Netanya on the spot. Jenny was overjoyed, the kids were excited. Joe, as usual was ambivalent. He had misgivings about leaving the kibbutz after all.

Maybe Bora is right. It isn't easy to uproot a whole family and start over again in the city. We have friends here, good jobs and are contributing to the defence of the country by living on this border kibbutz… but Jenny is so determined to leave. My marriage is at stake here. I'm not sure what to do.

Joe was worried about the old man, had to admit he felt some affection for him after all.

Chapter 27
GOODBYE AFIKEI KINNERET

A bright day in May. Driving back to the kibbutz after a second visit in Netanya, Joe reached the turn off by the Kinneret, and started the ascent up the snake road. He pulled the car over where there was a good view of the lake, its glistening waters reflecting the blue sky above them, the late afternoon wind off the lake carrying the familiar scent of figs from the Kibbutz Maagan plantation.

"Look, Jenny, at how glorious the view is here. We're leaving this beauty behind," Joe said, sadly.

"We can still come to visit, Joe, spend holidays in the area, go camping with the kids, like those people we passed down there on the way up."

"I suppose. It's getting dark, we'd better get back in the car and continue on our way home."

"Yes, you're right. I want to get the kids to bed at a reasonable hour this evening. Let's go!"

He put the radio on, but there was just static. He turned it off again. They drove on silently, each contemplating the seriousness of their decision to leave.

Is this the right thing to do?

"You know, Jen, we've had ten good years on the kibbutz. We have friends, the kids have friends. It isn't going to be easy to leave, and it won't be easy starting again in a new place," he told her.

"I know Joe, but if we don't do it now, when we're older it'll be even harder to move and start again. We both have higher education, work skills and connections like Rivka, and Bora. That won't last forever. They're old. You have a job offer now too. Now's the time to do it... and with our parents' help we can do it financially, I'm sure."

"I guess you're right. We're going to need their help. Leaving the kibbutz without that would be impossible. We'd leave with nothing in our pockets otherwise."

"But you do agree that now's the time?" she asked, noticing his doubtful look.

Joe hesitated a long time before replying "Yes."

The hardest step of all was telling Selma. She had helped them so much and they had grown to love her as part of the family. But they did it.

The next afternoon after work, Jenny invited Selma over for coffee. The apartment smelled of freshly baked chocolate cake as they talked about the children and their education, about the infighting between Peres and Rabin over Labour Party leadership, the problems of the kibbutz movement. Jenny winked at him in encouragement and Joe put down his still steaming coffee and got to the point, his hand gripping the table as he spoke:

"Selma, I know when we told you that we're thinking of leaving you didn't believe us, you thought our visits to explore possibilities weren't serious, but this time we've made up our minds."

Selma's face had turned red. She put down her half-eaten piece of cake.

"About what?"

"Joe has a job offer in Netanya. He's going to take it. We'll finish the school year and then move this coming summer," Jenny explained. She was crying as she spoke.

Selma faced Joe, looked him directly in the eyes. "Is that true?"

"Yes." Joe nodded solemnly as he spoke.

It was a painful moment; Joe watched the expression on Selma's broad face go through a rainbow of emotions as it went from anger to sadness to acceptance. Then, she broke into a huge smile, beaming her usual kindness at them.

Jenny and Joe smiled back at her awkwardly.

"Well, I wish you well. I guess you need a change, but you'll be back. You should know that Afikei Kinneret will always be your home."

The kibbutz buzzed for a while, then things died down and

the pilgrimage of friends to their room began.

Dov came to say goodbye, Harry came, even Nachshon and Shoshana had a farewell afternoon coffee with them. Soon everyone went back to normal day-to-day interactions as if they weren't about to leave.

There were also those, like Jenny's boss, and Maurice, the gardener, who stopped talking to them. That hurt.

Summer came. The day of parting finally came.

They stood next to the van they had rented, packed high with their belongings, the old partisan coat thrown in as well, despite Jenny's protests. The kids were impatient to go, having already said their goodbyes.

Selma accompanied them to the car, their other friends who were at work had said their goodbyes the night before.

"Good luck you two!"

"Selma, you'll come visit, won't you?" said Jenny.

"You'll be back before I have to do that."

"We'll see. We'll miss you," Joe said.

"I'll miss you too."

"I will miss this beautiful place," Jenny added.

"Of course. I will too. That view is something special, and you know I planted a lot of those trees over there. And the rose bushes there. And that lawn..."

"Joe, please stop."

"Yeah, you two should get going already!"

Hugs, kisses, tears. They left.

Joe watched as the kibbutz's concrete buildings disappeared in the rear-view mirror while Jenny played "I spy with my little eye" with the kids. They drove down the snake route towards the lake, passed the place of the accident those many years before, and on towards Tiberias.

Over the coming years their visits became less and less frequent, then they turned into yearly greetings on the phone and occasional camping trips nearby. The kids made new friends.

The river of life swept them on in its powerful current.

Chapter 28
CITY LIFE

They settled in Netanya and found schools they liked there. Joe took the biology teaching job in a local high school, and some agricultural advisory work in moshavim nearby. Kibbutz Maagan Michael gave him some consultancy work as well. Jenny got a job at the local hospital... but they weren't happy there either.

They lived in Netanya less than a year, then moved on to Kfar Saba. Life was much better there, the kids were growing, Joe found work teaching in a college, completed a doctorate, Jenny became a senior nurse, completed an M.Sc. in Public Health.

Rina was becoming a little woman, and an excellent dancer. Eitan played recorder and was an A-grade pupil. Each of the kids had found their niche, despite the upheaval of moving twice.

Letters from Australia, annual visits to Rivka on her kibbutz, the family settled into a routine despite the national emergencies and politics.

Then a phone call came from Melbourne.

Eva told Joe that Yanosh was seriously ill. Eva called again two days later, before Joe could arrange a flight. She cried into the phone as Joe listened stunned, knowing it was bad news. Yanosh had died. Eva explained that he had an undiscovered cancer of the pancreas, he went fast.

Joe missed the funeral, but flew to Melbourne to join his mother and Lily, who sat Shiva at home in mourning for seven days, according to the Jewish custom. He said the Kaddish prayer as requested, though it didn't mean much to him.

"Yitgadal VaYitkadash..."

Eva wept.

She was silent through most of the week, barely speaking to anyone, looking blankly at everyone as people came and went to console her. Her eyes were red and there were dark circles under them.

Lily cuddled her mother protectively. She looked so much like her, Joe thought. Same colour eyes, same thick glasses, and same wavy hair. Eva's was completely white now, but Lily's was auburn, like her mother's hair had been when she was younger, when he was a boy in Melbourne, and like Jenny's hair too.

Maybe the similarity between Jenny and Mum had attracted me to her? I've never thought of that before.

He knew that he didn't look like either of his parents himself. He had been told many times that he looked nothing like Lily either.

He saw that Lily was crying too, but he couldn't cry. He felt inadequate, unable to feel much, numbed, but he held his mother's hand, tried to be supportive of her, and of his sister in their mourning.

Joe saw Judy, Adam, and other childhood friends at the Shiva. They were kind, but he felt alienated after so many years living so far away. He resented their simple, uncritical Zionism. He judged them harshly. Too harshly, he realized later. He had his own doubts, but... but he still loved the country, and appreciated their support. They didn't really understand his life in Israel, living their comfortable suburban lives in Melbourne.

He realized that he was struggling with anger at his father. He remembered Yanosh's stubborn resistance to anything to do with Jewish religion that had prevented him from celebrating a bar mitzvah like his friends, Yanosh's relentless criticism of Israel and Zionism, his bitter opposition to his decision to go on aliya, his refusal to visit him on his kibbutz. He felt his father was always distant and disapproving, that Yanosh didn't accept him for who he was.

But he was his dad; he was after all the only father he had, and he knew there was love there in their relationship... however much it was hidden.

Then he returned to his life in Israel.

Eva visited twice more, always accompanied by Rivka.

His mother now looked so old, frail, but she came. He was nurtured by her love. Jenny loved her. Eva enjoyed the two grandchildren. She lit up when playing with them. They spent a summer in Melbourne with her, came back full of stories of fun with their grandmother.

Then Eva, too, died. Of old age, they said. In her sleep.

This time Joe and Jenny both attended the funeral, as did her friend Rivka, despite her advanced age. They flew home to Tel Aviv together, listened to Rivka's stories about their youth in the D.P. camp in Germany, about the strange relationship they all had with Bora. "Especially your mother," she told Joe. He didn't understand what she meant at the time.

Chapter 29

A Dream

A silent wood, in the snow.

Bora appeared from behind trees, carrying a rifle. He was wearing the fur coat. Joe recognized it right away. He looked angry, was yelling something, a command, but Joe could not hear the words.

There were others behind him, old people, women, children in rags, yellow stars sewn into their clothes... Only Bora did not have a yellow star on his chest.

They were running, terrified.

Bombs exploding, the sound of machine gun fire, flares. German soldiers were approaching fast from behind the little running crowd, shooting.

Screams. One fell. Another, and another. Soon all that Joe could see were bleeding bodies in pink snow.

Joe was helpless. All the people before him, including Bora, had been killed.

Silence.

Joe awoke, startled, wiping sweat off his face and neck.

What was that? Was I dreaming?

Jenny looked over at him and asked: "What's the matter, Joe?"

"Nothing," Joe said, blowing her a kiss. He felt shocked, unable to sleep again, but he did.

Jenny sat up, worried about Joe. She couldn't get back to sleep, so she got up, slid into slippers, wrapped herself in her fleecy green robe, went over to the window and glimpsed outside.

There was a blue, rotating light below. It was a police car. A man was standing down there, facing the wall. He wore blue jeans and a white t-shirt. Two policemen were frisking him, another sat in the police car, smiling as he watched them.

"Joe, wake up!" she suddenly called out, startling Joe.

He sat up rubbing his eyes, "Why? What's the matter?"

Jenny insisted: "Come here and look at what's happening down there in the street."

"What's up?" I want to sleep. Why don't you come back to bed?"

"No, Joe, come look. There are police down there. They've stopped a man. They are frisking him."

Joe got out of bed at last and came over to see what she was talking about.

"It's nothing, Jenny. Just another Arab car thief, that's all," he said.

Jenny, cried out, pointing: "Look! They're hitting him. He's bleeding."

"Let's shut the window and close the blind. It's none of our business!"

That sin of inaction haunted him. He couldn't sleep now. Wheels whirled around in his head, bad memories:

The Lebanon war... Going into action... Getting wounded...

Bora's visit to the hospital, his weird smile as he stood by his bed...

...Sabra and Shatila... counting the dead who died in Sharon's political war...

Bora was part of all that evil... He'd supported the war. Was it because of his truuma, the Holocaust?

He remembered the song he and his friends sang up there:

Re'ed Aleinu Aviron,
Kakh Otanu LeLevanon,
Sham nilahem bishvil Sharon
veNahzor Betoch Aron"

Come down plane,
Take us to Lebanon,
There we'll fight for Sharon,
and come home in a coffin.

Innocent people were killed in Lebanon. I was part of that. I remember the scenes of bombed villages, fleeing refugees. Maybe this Arab outside was the child of refugees too.

There's so much injustice, hatred in this country. I've got to stop listening to the news, stop reading newspapers, and live, blocking out all this stuff. But I can't do it.

He couldn't stop caring, felt responsible, wanted peace.

Chapter 30
GUARD DUTY IN KETZIOT

Joe sat in a guard tower in Ketziot, on a cold winter desert night wrapped in his fur coat struggling to stay awake. He'd run out of tea and was bored. His turn-of-duty was long, seemingly endless, and uneventful, like so many others over the years as a reservist soldier. He was exhausted, looking forward to the arrival of the next guard to relieve him to get some sleep.

Suddenly sirens sounded. Cars were moving, screeching, the night was lit up by spotlights. He heard yelling.

"A prisoner has escaped!" someone yelled below.

Oh no! Now I'm stuck in this bloody guard tower!

Soldiers were running about, down below but no one came to relieve him nor did anyone tell him what was happening.

Two hours later he was startled to hear from the ladder below: "OK, Joe, you can come down now. They caught him."

Relieved, he came down from the guard tower at last, started walking towards his tent, hands deep in the warm coat pockets. On the way, he saw a bizarre scene:

Two soldiers were dragging a prisoner, with limp, broken arms hanging on either side of him, along through the sand. Joe followed behind them to see the man thrown into one of the solitary confinement cubicles. It was an ugly, grey concrete bloc with a slit as its window for food and observation.

Joe went to the infirmary to Josh, the religious medic on duty whom he had befriended.

"The escaped prisoner... help him! His arms are broken, he needs medical attention," Joe said, gasping.

Josh phoned the new prison doctor and begged him to come.

"You woke me to attend to an escaped Arab prisoner? Let the bastard suffer, let the Arabusch learn his lesson. Call back in the morning. Good night!" the doctor growled into the phone.

"Wait a minute! This is an emergency. He needs medical treatment. And there's a Red Cross visit scheduled for tomorrow morning!" Josh answered. Josh winked at Joe.

"Red Cross visit in the morning? Why didn't anyone tell me! OK. I am coming," the doctor said.

"A little white lie never hurt, especially if you want someone else to be a mensch for a change!" Josh explained.

Later in his tent trying to sleep, Joe thought about the scene.

Did I do anything? Did I change anything? This sort of thing probably happens all the time down here. I helped that one prisoner, who received medical treatment, saved him from further abuse, maybe I've pinched a conscience or two, but nothing's changed. How many decent people like Josh are there in the army, after all? Most people try to keep their heads low, and not stir up trouble for themselves. Is this just so I can feel heroic or righteous or something?

But he decided to get involved anyway. He could not just sit at home now. Something had gone wrong in Israeli society, and he had to respond. He joined the army veterans protest group called "Breaking the Silence".

Chapter 31
BEIT SAHOUR, 1988

Joe called Jenny from his reserve duty to tell her he was OK. He told her he was in a place called Ketziot, guarding a detention camp for Palestinian terrorists, that he'd be home the next Shabbat and would then tell her more. There'd been some excitement, but he couldn't talk about it on the phone.

That same evening Jenny sat in a circle of Israeli and Palestinian women in the living room of a Christian Palestinian family in Beit Sahour, a suburb of Bethlehem. Seated on low wicker seats with brightly coloured cushions, steaming tea in front of them on small tables, they went around the circle introducing themselves, each one telling something about herself, about her family.

First one, then another Palestinian woman gave their name and expressed their hopes for peace, while detailing their sufferings under Israeli occupation.

About halfway around the circle a woman called Aiyisha suddenly said: "My husband is in jail, in the Ketziot detention camp. They came in the middle of the night to take him."

After that, one after another said the same.

Increasingly anxious Jenny waited for her turn to talk. Eventually it came. Everyone looked at her, expectant.

"Well... I'm from Canada, but I've been living in Israel 14 years now. I'm married. I'm a nurse. My husband is an agricultural advisor but now he's in the army, doing reserve duty. He too, like your menfolk, is in Ketziot. He is a guard there, but we want this to end, dream of peace, too."

The other women looked at her in shock, she squirmed under their angry gaze until one of them laughed and said: "Well, we're all literally in this together, aren't we?"

Jenny relaxed, but she didn't quite see the humour in their situation. She went home disturbed by what she'd heard there.

Two days later Bora called. Jenny answered.

"Hello Mrs. Kamens. This is Bora."

"Oh. Hello. You are looking for Joe I suppose? He is in the army – reserve duty."

"I know that Mrs. Kamens. I know where he is. I wanted to have a word with you this time, not Joe."

"I'm surprised. What's this about?"

"I just want to warn you about your recent meetings with a certain group of women."

"What?"

"The Palestinian ladies you have been meeting with are enemies of Israel. You should stay away from them."

Just like with Joe, Bora didn't say goodbye. Just hung up.

When Joe came home from his reserve duty and Jenny told him about this phone call. He was furious.

"What right does he have telling us who we should or shouldn't talk to!? I will call him and tell him to lay off us."

"No Joe. Let it go."

He didn't call him, but he did ask Jenny to be careful whom she told about her meetings with Palestinian women, not to mention it on the phone.

"We're being listened to," he explained. "We are under surveillance."

Chapter 32
MEETING BORA AGAIN

Then a letter arrived from Lily. After Eva's Shiva, Joe and Jenny had returned to Israel. Lily was left to take care of things, to sell the house, organize her mother's things and decide what to do with them. She wrote that she had come across correspondence between Eva and Bora. She promised to call and explain what she'd found. They set a date and time for her call.

Lily's call came. "Listen Joe, I've something to tell you. Sit down. Brace yourself. You're not going to believe this."

Joe sat down, as asked, and said: "OK, I'm listening."

"They were having an affair." Lily's voice was quivering as she said the words.

Joe didn't understand and asked, "What are you talking about, Lily?"

"I told you that you wouldn't believe it. Mum and Bora…"

"I can't believe it. When?"

"It's true. I found their love letters. I'll photocopy them and send you copies. You'll see. I couldn't believe it myself until I read them."

The copies arrived in the express mail a week later. Jenny watched him read letter after letter, intensely, at one sitting after work that day. Joe recognized his mother's handwriting immediately and figured Bora's from the brief messages he'd written over the years. The same handwriting, neat and tight, with a final, long stroked, letter, in flight across the page, a flourish of ink.

Joe had known nothing about Bora and his mother's affair, an affair that, he now understood, almost destroyed his parent's marriage. Sister Lily's disturbing letter had piqued his curiosity. He wanted to find out more. Joe felt ambivalent about it, but he knew he would have to meet Bora again, to find out what had happened.

It would take half a day to travel up north to Beit Alfa. He would have to stay overnight and return the next day, taking a day or two off work, leaving Jenny to deal with the kids alone. She agreed to it, but he knew it would not be easy, that he was asking a lot of her. He would leave her the car, of course, to transport the kids to school, and their after-school activities and all that.

He hadn't been able to sleep since reading the letters the day before yesterday. He had torn one up in a fit of rage but could still remember every word:

Dearest Eva,

I miss you more than words can say. I long to see you again, to hold you in my embrace. Your home should be here with me, not there in the boring suburb of Caulfield in Melbourne with Yanosh... You are so far, so far away my love...

Bora.

Joe was determined to go and confront Bora about the past.

Now I remember that Bora looked at me in a strange way whenever we met, tried to protect me, touched me as if we were family, treated me paternally, despite his usually gruff manner... shared his partisan memories with me in Belarus... He told me once that I looked like my mother. How could I not have suspected anything?! It all makes sense now. I'll call him right away... set up a visit... I want to know the truth.

"Hello Bora?"

He felt his own nervousness as he waited for the response.

He heard some heavy breathing, then a low, familiar voice half whispered half croaked into the phone...

"Hello. Yes, it's Bora. Who's this?"

"It's Joe. Joe Kamens."

"Oh. Hello Yossi! How are you?"

"Bora, I have been wanting to come visit you for a while now. Tomorrow, I have an opportunity to do it. Will you be home tomorrow?"

"Yes, I'm home. Shifra will be here too. We'd be delighted to see you. It's warm here, but not too hot. No other guests now. No problem at all. Just come. We will take you swimming in the local stream. Or you can spend time at the Sachneh."

As Bora spoke, the image of that sparkling natural lake surrounded by green lawns and trees appeared in his mind – memory of pleasant swims in warm waters.

"Great. I will catch a bus tomorrow morning," Joe said.

"Wait a minute, Yossi. This does seem very sudden. And in the middle of the week... Umh, why not come for the weekend? Is something the matter?" Bora responded.

"Bora, eh... I need to talk to you about something."

"You can do that on the phone, can't you?"

"No, I want to speak to you in person."

"Well, OK. You are always welcome."

"Great. See you tomorrow then!"

The next morning Joe got dressed and packed a few things – a change of clothes, his swimming gear, a sandwich, a couple of pieces of fruit, a bottle of water. He downed his coffee, donned his Aussie sun hat, and headed for the bus stop. The clanking sound of his partially broken sandal was annoying, but he did his best to ignore it as he strode down the road.

The bus, green and almost empty, came soon. The gruff, moustache-adorned driver took his money, supplied him with a ticket, sharply pulled the bus out of the bus stop. Joe was thrown backwards but blocked his fall and angrily sat down in the front seat, next to the window. The sign said something about being reserved for invalids. He ignored it. Curled up to the window and fell asleep.

"Beit She'an! We are in Beit She'an," the driver told him. "You get off here and catch a local bus now."

Confused and still sleepy, Joe half-slid, half-walked down the aisle of the bus, then down the steps. He looked around. A dusty, smelly platform. Two stationary buses. A small group of long-skirted, chattering schoolgirls, and a bored-looking teacher was what he saw. Beyond that, a row of white stone buildings, a tree or two, and the quiet of a small town. An occasional old, sometimes beaten-up, and rusty car passed. He found his way to the ticket seller's window.

"When's the next bus to kibbutz Beit Alfa?"

"There's a bus at 1:15 this afternoon. 10 shekels."

"That's the earliest bus?"

"Yes. 10 shekels please." Joe paid.

It was only 12 o'clock. He had an hour to kill. He'd go for lunch...

■■■

No one knew what he had died of. His wife, Shifra, found him sitting, dead, in his favourite rocking chair under a palm frond covered shelter (a sukka) beside his modest Beit Alfa home. His hand still held the morning newspaper, Al Hamishmar, meaning "On Guard", the headline telling of some government coalition crisis or other. The newspaper, blowing in the breeze, was the only movement to be seen. His head was tilted forward at a strange angle, his eyes staring blankly out at the world, no expression of irony or cunning there any longer. His mouth had fallen open, revealing the gap where his false teeth had been. They had fallen and were lying on the grass below the chair. His body was cold.

Chapter 33

BORA'S FUNERAL

Joe parked his car near the Mount Herzl cemetery entrance and walked in. He continued through the entrance arch into an open concrete compound with flags flying from several poles. He then walked through some bushes and a row of trees until he reached the military graves.

Joe walked on until he reached the funeral site. There he watched as Bora's coffin, draped in the national flag, was lowered into the grave. Shots were fired into the air. The soil was shovelled into the pit, and then heaped over the grave after the hole had been filled. Stones were placed there, some wreaths of flowers from the Mossad, from government offices for which Bora had worked.

The poet and former partisan fighter Abba Kovner said a few flowery words of eulogy that Joe could barely understand; a white bearded old rabbi recited the *El Malei Rachamim* prayer for the dead before the crowd of mostly blank faces. Only a few responded with a*men* which didn't surprise him considering that few had covered their heads, and then everyone left. Rivka, who did respond with amen, came, and others he recognized from Kibbutz Lochamei HaGetaot, as well as a representative of Yad Vashem. Sasha was there and Vladimir was too, towering over everyone.

Vladimir came over to Joe and gave him a bear hug.

That scent, the smell of the man's aftershave… I recognize it.

"Do you remember me?" Vladimir asked.

"Yes. Of course," Joe answered. "You're the only Olympic medallist I've ever met! How are you, Vladimir?"

"I'm OK, but sad at losing Bora. He was a good man, helped many people like me."

"Yes, I know, there were so many questions I wanted to ask him about the past, but now that's impossible."

"You were close to him?"

"Not exactly, and there was another side to him, apart from

the good things he did..."

Vladimir nodded.

He was aware of his own ambivalence regarding Bora but didn't want to talk about it any further. "Nice to see you again," Joe said.

Vladimir strode away, head bent.

The rabbi led Bora's widow aside and spoke with her in whispers. Joe wondered whether it was appropriate to approach with his secret at the funeral, but decided not to do so.

Joe couldn't hear what was being said. The rabbi's assistant asked the crowd to form two lines through which they would walk and be consoled before leaving the cemetery. He obliged and walked over to join one of the lines of people. As he walked, he felt a hand touching his shoulder from behind. He turned to see the unfamiliar face of an older blonde woman with light, blue-green eyes.

"You don't know me," she said. I am a friend of your father's from long ago. I have seen your picture before. Now that I can see you more clearly, I see you don't look like him. I suppose you take after your mother."

"Who are you?"

"I am Ursula. From Norway... Oslo."

"Yes. And?"

"And I have something for you. Bora spent time with me in Oslo. He told me about your parents, about their relationship in Poland after the war. He had a great deal of respect for Yanosh and his writing. Read his articles over the years. He related to him as he might to a brother, and he thought of you as almost a nephew... Here, this should be yours now."

The woman handed him a small paper-wrapped object. He noticed how scarred the hand that held it was, *scars from fire* he thought. He took the parcel and weighed it in his hands. It felt heavy.

"Thank you..." he began to say, but she had already walked off.

He opened the little parcel. Inside he found a black metal

240

replica of a human skull attached to a silver chain. There were two white S.S. lightning bolts on the forehead. There was a word inscribed under it. It read Schutzstaffel. Inside, he also found a small rolled up piece of paper that he carefully unrolled and read:

A gift for my friend, Yanosh Kaminski, from the other world.
Joseph Borowski

Joe turned the medallion over in his hand in horror:

What is this? Is it a souvenir from the days when they assassinated S.S. men after the second world war? I don't want to keep this thing. It's spooky. Maybe I'll donate it to some museum, like the one at Kibbutz Lochamei HaGetaot or Yad Vashem? I'm happy Jenny didn't come. She would've been upset by this. Is there no escape from this stuff!

Joe walked over to the fresh grave as everyone began to leave. He placed a stone on it.

Goodbye, Bora, forever. Rest in peace.

Joe had never been to the military cemetery on Mount Herzl before. As he walked away from Bora's grave, he began to look around.

The rows of soldiers' graves were in neat parallel lines, each the same, each inscribed with army cliches and I.D.F. symbols. He read some names and ages engraved on the first few graves: "Private Joseph Cohen, aged 18; Corporal Avraham Levy, aged 21; Private Yigal Abutbul, aged 19; Divsha Recanati, aged 18; Lieutenant Tamar Goldstein, aged 20; Captain Oded Avrami, aged 22".

Joe froze when he read that name, looked at the grave again, placed a stone on it and continued walking, wondering whether that was the grave of Rivka's son. The dates were all recent, the soil still fresh from having been disturbed in digging these graves. All had neat piles of stones on them, there were lit memorial candles in little windows in front of most of the graves, fresh red and blue flowers lay on many of them. Oded had been killed years before. It must be a different Oded Avrami.

This is a depressing, disturbing place. So many young people whose lives were cut short for the country. My kids will have to go to the army too... no, don't go there! Never want to come here again.

He stopped reading and walked on to a different section with older graves, also neatly laid out in rows, but he didn't read the names there. He smelled the burning wax coming from candles lit in the little glasses at the base of some of the graves, saw the flowers and stones, bright recently placed blooms, faded, wilted, flowers, shiny stones of marble, dark granite pieces.

Here and there an old man or woman or some children with a young mother stood silently by a grave. A couple of young soldiers, carrying weapons and looking serious, walked past him.

Joe thought again about his children, that they too would have to go to the army. The conflict here seemed never ending. Was there no hope of peace in this country? Would it never end?

■■■

But Joe just couldn't escape the man. He saw Bora sometimes in his dreams. Short and stocky, bald with two white tufts of hair on either side of his head above large ears. Bora would smile or wink at him, then disappear. He was always wearing his fur coat, his hands in his pockets.

Too many things had reminded him of the man in Israel. He had to get away, to get out of this crazy country and find peace again. He had emigrated from one of the most peaceful countries on earth and now had come to appreciate that, to understand his parents' love of the "sunburned country", had begun to connect with his being an Aussie himself.

But he couldn't return to Melbourne and his sister there, nor return to the Jewish community or his childhood friends from the Zionist youth group either. That would be too difficult, too distressing. He would have to move on, to find somewhere else to be himself, to recover himself and find some inner peace again. If he was single, he would have tried moving up north to Northern Queensland or the Northern Territory! Maybe he could have found work in Darwin, for instance? But who was he kidding! He had a family, a job, a home in Kfar Saba. He was anchored in Israel now.

He would have loved to start anew, to leave all the confusion and psychological anguish of Israel behind. He would have liked to live a simpler life, to have lived as an ordinary Australian, without the burden of that terrible past, without the weight of Jewish history pulling him down. He didn't need to let Israel and its crazy demands poison him any longer, and he wanted Bora, that strange ghost from his parents' journey out of Europe, to stay in his grave and stop haunting him. Now that he was dead, it was time Bora let go of Joe's soul.

Postscript
ANOTHER BURIAL

The coat lay in the boydem storage in their city home for a long time after they moved. It hadn't been touched in years. One day, before Pesach, Jenny pulled it down. She wanted to make room there to store old toys for future grandchildren now that the children had outgrown them, now that Eitan was going to the army.

It fell to the floor with a thump in a cloud of dust. It smelled. It lay there like an enormous dead animal. She sneezed.

It's time to get rid of this... to bury it, and with it, the past.

She picked up the fur coat to carry it outside, thinking it would eventually decompose in the garden and nurture future plant growth there, feed the flowers.

Before she had taken two steps, Joe came in from work. He looked at her in dismay.

"What do you have there?" he asked.

"Your old partisan coat. The one you used to wear as a kid, as a student, and when you first came to Israel. The one you tried to return to Bora. You would never let me get rid of it when I wanted to make room to store things," she replied.

"Oh, yeah. That coat. It's been lying there for years now, collecting dust."

"It stinks, Joe. I think it's time to get rid of it. I need the room up there for these toys."

"You're thinking about grandkids now?"

"Why not?"

"But the kids are still in school. That's way in the future!"

"Maybe... but we need the space... and this old bulky coat is in the way. Bora is dead now."

"I guess you are right. I'm never going to wear that smelly, moth-bitten old thing again."

"Now you are talking sensibly!"

"But it does make me feel sad to see it go. It is a piece of history you know."

"History? It's a reminder of a nightmare… a bit of Yad Vashem in the boydem. I've wanted to get rid of it for a long time now."

"Oh, it's not just about practical considerations like space for toys for our kids' kids? It's about your hang-ups, about avoiding and not dealing with the past!"

"You could say that. Bora's long dead now. They're all gone now… time to finally get rid of this thing."

Joe was surprised to find himself choking up, tears coming to his eyes, then rolling down his cheeks. He wiped them away.

She watched and waited for him to calm.

"OK, Jenny, let's do it together."

He took the fur coat from her, laid it across his arms, carried it out to the garden, and placed it on a barren spot. He returned with a spade and began to dig a hole for it.

"Yitgadal Veyitkadash…" Jenny joked, reciting the mourner's prayer, but Joe wasn't laughing.

"That's appropriate," Joe commented. He continued reciting what he remembered of the words of the prayer and saw that Jenny too had tears in her eyes. He hugged her.

They buried it, then went inside holding hands.

The ground was hard, rocky, but some grass grew there. The next spring some red anemones, purple rock roses and yellow marigolds appeared around that spot. The flowers waved in the warm eastern wind as it brought in the reddish dust of the first hamsin that year and then drops of dusty rain. Of the coat, only his memories remained.

THE AUTHOR

Yehiel Grenimann is the eldest child of two Polish Holocaust survivors.

After completing his MA in Holocaust Studies at the Hebrew University's Institute for Contemporary Jewry, he spent ten years in Holocaust education and was Director of the Ot Ve'Ed Institute in Jerusalem, where he focused on teaching teenagers, young adults, and educators about Jewish resistance during World War II.

Since receiving his rabbinical ordination from the Schechter Institute of Jewish Studies in 1991, he has worked as a rabbi and educator in the Masorti movement. For many years, he has been active in groups such as Tag Meir, Oz Veshalom and Rabbis for Human Rights.

Yehiel is the author of *Far Away From Where?*, published by Mazo Publishers, 2011.

Yehiel's following work has appeared in many publications:

"A Theological Confrontation with the Holocaust," *Et La'asot* (Journal of the Seminary of Judaic Studies and the Masorti Movement in Israel), Winter 1996 (in Hebrew).

Commentaries on weekly and festival Torah portions, in Hebrew and English. 1991-2023.

"Bitter Conflict – Can Judaism Bring Hope?" published in an anthology edited by Prof. Gerrie ter Haar, "Religion, Violence and Visions for Peace" (Brill Publishers, 2005).

"Letter From Jerusalem: Masorti Giyur", Conservative Judaism, Vol. 57, No. 4, Summer 2005 (Publication of the Rabbinical Assembly and J.T.S., New York).

"Purim In The Forest" (short story), in *The Beauty of the Story*, ed. Rosally Saltsman (Judaica Press, New York, 2009).

The chapter "The Seder" in *Far Away From Where?* was published in *JewishFiction.net* Volume 1, No. 3, February 24, 2011.

A long-time Jerusalem resident, he is married to Deborah and the father of four adult children, grandfather of seven.

FAR AWAY FROM WHERE?

A Prequel to
The Partisan's Coat

www.farawayfromwhere.com